IDEAS ON LIBERTY

Essays in Honor of
Paul L. Poirot

PAUL L. POIROT

IDEAS ON LIBERTY

Essays in Honor of
Paul L. Poirot

www.FEE.org   Mises.org

Thanks to Gary North,
the man responsible for this volume.

Reprinted by the Ludwig von Mises Institute
518 West Magnolia Avenue
Auburn, Alabama 36832
mises.org

ISBN: 978-1-61016-198-5

Contents

Foreword

DR. PAUL L. POIROT died at the age of ninety in 2006, and with his passing I lost one of my closest and best friends. Paul Poirot is remembered by most people as the thirty-year editor of *The Freeman*, the monthly journal published by the Foundation for Economic Education since 1956. But Paul Poirot was much more than just an editor to those of us who worked closely with him over the decades.

Dr. Poirot was an uncompromising proponent of the ideal concept of a free society and the Austrian economic theory perspective upon which an unhampered market process is founded. As Leonard Read, the founding president of FEE, liked to put it, "Paul doesn't leak!" And certainly Paul Poirot and his journal, *The Freeman*, never wavered from advancing the cause of individual liberty and the essential absolutes of private property and monetary freedom required for the achievement of a free market order.

Outwardly, Paul Poirot was a reticent man, but in his actions and professional efforts he was the most tenacious, competent, and organized man I've ever known. We became very close friends over almost a half century of his life, especially during the many years when our offices at FEE were across the hall from one other. He was my mentor and confident in all things during that era, and I count my blessings for the remarkable association we enjoyed together.

Among the essays in this festschrift for Dr. Poirot is Gary North's, "Jeremiah's Job." I cannot read that essay without thinking of Paul Poirot's determination and dedication through his editorial efforts with *The Freeman*. He devoted his intellectual skills for over thirty years consistently pursuing "Jeremiah's Job." And he did it knowing we were engaging in a rear-guard, losing action at that time!

A personal aside: One day back in the mid-1970's I mentioned how bleak our economic outlook seemed by our shrinking cohorts of principled devotees to the ideal concept of a free society, the banner under which FEE was founded in 1946. I was discouraged. Paul's immediate response was, "We have, indeed, lost much of our constituency." Whereupon, he immediately wrote one of his best essays, "He Gains Most Who Serves Best," for *The Freeman*. Now, that's tenacity and commitment!

Of course Leonard Read, FEE's founding president, is properly recognized as the guiding force for establishing FEE as a principled free market institution advancing the ideal concept of a free society, but it was *The Freeman* under the sole direction of Paul Poirot which provided the monthly message making the case for individual liberty and the private property order. Dr. Poirot was a master at transforming a promising essay by a new author into a highly readable and informative article. I know, since he took my first published effort in 1961, "Pithole," and gave it a meaningful conclusion which provided it the ending it needed. He quietly did this for hundreds of submitted essays, and only a few of us who worked with him were ever aware of the positive changes he added to those essays.

Paul Poirot was a master of the language. His letters were a delight to receive. His proficiency shown through in the pages of his journal, and made it a pleasure to indulge in the philosophical ideas contained therein. Paul Poirot was the "quiet force" which made this happen over the years. While Paul was the epitome of the perfect gentleman and blessed with a kind and thoughtful temperament, he was completely intolerant toward any deviation or compromise of the philosophy of individual freedom. He could spot philosophical flaws immediately, and such an essay would be gently rejected. While Leonard Read was the "founding rock" at FEE in those years, it was Paul Poirot who saw to it that "founding rock" never got compromised.

Both Paul and I shared an operational awareness that he handled much better than I. Many years ago Victor Milione of the Intercollegiate Studies Institute observed the difficulty for free market organizations to survive when they refused to become political, something FEE had avoided doing in its early days. Vic pointed out that people were becoming more interested in their immediate political plight than the intellectual pursuit of an ideal concept of a free society. To Paul Poirot's great credit as editor of *The Freeman*, he never yielded to any pressures to become political, even though many of FEE's board and supporters did. Paul Poirot wisely ignored this ominous change and pursued "Jeremiah's Job" as he always had. He was a truly principled and tenacious man!

The readings which follow reflect the legacy of Paul Poirot in his life-long pursuit of the philosophy of freedom. Almost all of the authors were long-time friends and associates of him, and all would agree Paul was an exceptional man. Beth Hoffman and I compiled this festschrift in honor of Dr. Poirot upon his retirement in 1987, and it was one of the most pleasant endeavors we ever undertook. The essays are original, outstanding, and worth reading. I'm deeply indebted to both Gary North and Lew Rockwell at the Mises Institute for making this book available in print again.

—ROBERT G. ANDERSON

July, 2012

Introduction

PAUL L. POIROT was born in Illinois farm country and received his bachelor's degree in agriculture from The University of Illinois in 1936. He went on to Cornell in Ithaca, New York, and received his Ph.D. in agricultural economics in 1940. Following stints at the Office of Price Administration and as an economist at a feed, seed, and fertilizer cooperative in Ithaca, he joined the staff of FEE in 1949.

Dr. Poirot edited many of the "In Brief" pamphlets which were the primary releases in the first decade of FEE's existence. His monograph on Social Security, "The Pension Idea," explored in detail the concepts of individual security and property and why we cannot look to the "false charity of governmental subsidy."

When The Foundation began publishing *The Freeman* on a monthly basis in 1956, Paul Poirot was tapped as editor. It was a good choice. As a writer, he was an exact thinker. As a reader, he was thorough. As a man, he was modest. These traits, combined with sound judgment and firm adherence to principle, made Paul Poirot an astute editor.

Paul Poirot's real work was largely unseen. Readers saw only the finished issue of *The Freeman* each month. What they did not see was his voluminous correspondence with authors-encouraging the newcomer who showed promise, delicately rejecting an unsuitable manuscript, or firmly explaining to a free-lancer that his manuscript was somewhat outside our "rather narrow scope of free market economics and limited government."

In addition to his *Freeman* chores, Paul Poirot oversaw the book publication and resale program, handling inventory and promotion and all the other details that accompany bookselling. He edited all of Leonard Read's FEE-published books, as well as hundreds of issues of *Notes from FEE* and a variety of brochures, monographs, and other publications.

In a sense, this anthology is an extension of Paul Poirot's *Freeman* work. The writers of these essays have all contributed to *The Freeman*. They have come to know and respect Paul Poirot both as editor and as friend.

The themes that run through the essays in this collection-the future of freedom, private property, individualism, morality, prices and pricing, the rule of law, central planning, labor and employment, classical liberalismare themes that are familiar to faithful *Freeman* readers. But each author, with each article, brings a fresh perspective, a new idea, something that may not have been said in quite the same way before. Through constant reinforcement of basic principles, *The Freeman* has established itself as an uncompromising voice of liberty.

As we continue our search for improved ways to explore and explain ideas on liberty, we are grateful that we have had the benefit of Paul Poirot's example. We hope we have learned our lessons well.

—BETH A. HOFFMAN

September, 1987

The Ever-Present Danger

BY ROBERT G. ANDERSON

AN EXPANDING community of individuals, given adequate time and proper values, will eventually become a civilization. The ultimate structure of these civilizations, however, can never be known because a multitude of forces will interact in their development. There is no way that the process which brought them into existence can ever be identified or evaluated in advance.

In contrast to socialist planners, those who wish to advance a free society clearly understand this point and would not presume to formulate any outcome for a social order. Their knowledge of the freedom philosophy commits them to nurturing those processes necessary for maximizing the freedom of choice for each individual member of society.

A free society, which is based on the moral imperatives of human liberty and private property, is presented as the ideal process for a social order because such a system creates the best arrangement for individuals to pursue their own personal welfare. In recognition of this fact, it is vitally important that methods for advancing a free society be formulated in such a way as to ensure that this objective is achieved.

Friedrich Hayek warned us almost twenty years ago that our primary commitment should be "the defense of our civilization against intellectual error." In that same address he observed that ". . . we differ not so much on ultimate values, but on the effective means of achieving them."

The desire to achieve a better quality of life for more people is a universal goal of all individuals of good will. The choice of means by which to achieve this goal is what divides them. Differences in ideas, many of which are founded on "intellectual error," lead inexorably to radically different methods for accomplishing similar goals.

Modern socialism has been a tragic case in point. The twentieth century has witnessed the implementation of a multitude of socialist intellectual errors. Because of the persistence of the fallacious notion that a better society could be prefabricated by human planners in a socialist mold, this century has witnessed an imposed poverty and human misery on an unprecedented scale. The result is that those who seek a more humane world are no longer able to ignore these failures nor the vast amount of literature which has completely repudiated these socialist ideas.

Yet, the knowledge of socialism's failures has not opened our minds to the better idea of freedom nor freed us from the fallacies of socialism. Instead, we must now contend with a mutation of socialism, a more "pragmatic" socialism that purportedly incorporates "market" principles into a socialist structure.

A "Pragmatic Socialism"?

Those who would graft such superficial changes on to an otherwise fundamentally flawed system have not repudiated the socialist idea that some individuals should forcibly exercise control over other individuals. We have indeed a very significant threat that this new "pragmatic socialism," utilizing market-type devices, will replace the failed socialist planning of the past.

This idea of a new "pragmatic socialism" is not originating only among socialist theoreticians. It is gaining much support from proponents of the free market as well. Free market economists who have failed to recognize the importance of safeguarding the moral absolutes of human liberty and private property often propose and welcome interventionist programs in the belief that they can mitigate the greater harm which has been caused by past socialist economic planning.

It is difficult to criticize such behavior by free market proponents. Given that there are only two kinds of government intervention in the economy (bad and worse), their desire to make things less bad by supporting the lesser of two evils is a rather typical reaction. But it does not follow that less bad programs to replace worse programs will ever lead to the free society.

Efforts to ameliorate the harmful effects of socialism by substituting more efficient interventionist programs is a serious mistake in strategy. When such activity violates the philosophical ideal of an unhampered market economy by desecrating private property rights and individual freedom of choice, it is a certainty that those proposals will never lead us to a free society. Instead, such efforts only serve to transform free market economists into "government efficiency experts," and prolong the harms caused by the socialist planning.

Ludwig von Mises pointed out that the end result of such socialist tampering is to create more government intervention to correct the ill effects of earlier government intervention. The difference today is that we must now witness these past socialist errors being committed by so-called advocates of a free market.

Today, more ominous than ever before, is the ever-present danger resulting from our inability to identify properly our "intellectual error." That error is the idea that it is appropriate to use government force to modify individual behavior and to politicalize private economic resources. Most important of all is the failure to understand that it is human liberty rather than economic efficiency which is the ultimate goal of the free society.

The importance of protecting human liberty and private property as moral absolutes has not been firmly grasped. The result is that strategies have been formulated which violate either freedom of choice, the property rights of an individual, or both. Such practices are taking us further from the free society and, in the process, creating a greater likelihood that all of us may someday be living in a "pragmatic socialist" society.

The incorporation of privatization policies, market structured allocation devices, or taxation provisions only increases the presence of the state in our lives whenever their adoption compromises human liberty and private property rights. Such government programs do not bring us back to freedom. Rather, they ensure the continuance of socialist ideas by entrenching the state more securely in its sovereign role over society.

Utilizing market-type devices, this modified form of "pragmatic socialism" may possibly realize what pure socialism could never have achieved— a command society with an omnipresent state exercising control over the citizenry. Even more ominous is the possibility that such a social order may survive for a lengthy time because of its use of more efficient market-type devices to strengthen its power over society.

Failing to understand the importance of remaining consistent to the principles of human liberty and private property is one of the most dangerous risks we encounter in our efforts to realize the free society. The temptation to deviate momentarily from the ideal concept of a completely unhampered market economy in order to gain some small victory over socialism is an ever-present danger.

Such temptations are typically attractive because they seem so reasonable. The opportunity for an immediate success often seems worth the price of a slight infringement on human liberty and private property. This is especially true when such proposals attract much public attention and appear to be politically feasible. The consequence of such reasoning, of course, is the eventual demise of the free society.

Advancing a free society requires a strategy which consistently applies the moral absolutes of human liberty and private property to any proposed endeavor. Dr. Paul Poirot never deviated from these ideals in his thirty years as managing editor of *The Freeman*. Until others fully understand and practice his kind of principled action, the cause of liberty will never be advanced.

Good intentions built on socialist ideas have exacted an awesome toll on our historical process. It is time that we begin to build our future on the ideals of a free society—human liberty and private property. The result will be a life of peace, harmony, and prosperity for all future generations to know and enjoy.

Mr. Anderson is Vice President of Operations at The Foundation for Economic Education.

Ebenezer Scrooge and the Free Society

by Howard Baetjer Jr.

Behaving in a self-interested manner does not mean disregarding others. On the contrary, because we are social beings who depend on, and often care deeply about many others around us, a sound attention to our self-interest must include a great deal of concern for others.

However true we may see this to be on a moment's reflection, many of us often lose sight of it, especially in our political and economic thinking. Particularly in regard to the free economy, a vague equating of selfishness and capitalism often infects people's thinking. The very word capitalism brings to many minds grim visions of ruthless characters damning the public interest or selling their mothers for farthings.

The archetype of the antisocial capitalist is Ebenezer Scrooge of Charles Dickens' classic tale, "A Christmas Carol." In Dickens' words, "Oh! But he was a tight-fisted hand at the grindstone, Scrooge! a squeezing, wrenching, grasping, scraping, clutching, covetous old sinner! Hard and sharp as flint, from which no steel had ever struck out generous fire; secret, and self-contained, and solitary as an oyster."

As many who attack the market would have it, Scrooge embodies the spiritual ruin of capitalism; he is the type toward which all capitalists tend. Indeed, I have a dear friend who jibes at my free market sympathies by quoting Scrooge's attitude about Christmas donations for the poor: "Are there no prisons? Are there no workhouses?"

It is as if he believes that supporting the free market means forswearing kindness, as if simply entering the competitive whirl of business contaminates individuals with an attitude of competitiveness—or rather of strife—that poisons their relationships, distorts their perspective, and destroys their feeling for the brotherhood of man.

The widespread notion that free markets are corrupting is rooted at least in part in the innocent truism that for the market to work people must act according to self-interest. Without the motivation of self-interest, there would be no profit seeking, no price competition, no production and exchange. True enough, the market requires self-interested behavior.

But many make an illogical leap from this truism to a falsehood: that if one is self-interested, one cannot be other-interested. Many see an either/or choice. Scrooge can care about Scrooge, or he can care about others: the poor, his clerk Bob Cratchit, Cratchit's family, including lame Tiny Tim, and so on. He cannot do both.

Supporters of economic liberty will win to their cause very few people who believe in this notion. As long as they see self-interest to be at odds with cherished values of generosity and fellow-feeling, people will not embrace a political economy based on self-interest. Thus a task for lovers of liberty is to point out that self-interest and interest in others are not at odds, that in fact they go together.

They do. In fact, that is one of the main lessons "A Christmas Carol" teaches. The point of the story is that Ebenezer Scrooge, the archetypal "greedy capitalist," becomes immeasurably happier when and because he gives up his selfishness and becomes generously involved with those around him. There is no suggestion that he gives up his capitalism; in fact, Dickens tells us that he is at his desk early the day after Christmas. He just broadens his other activities and ends.

A quick recapitulation for those who may have forgotten the story: After refusing his nephew's invitation to Christmas dinner, refusing to donate anything to a Christmas fund for the poor, driving away a boy singing Christmas carols, and only grudgingly granting Bob Cratchit Christmas Day off, Scrooge goes home to a harrowing night. He is visited by the ghost of his old partner, and then in succession the ghosts Christmas Past, Christmas Present, and Christmas Yet To Come. The ghosts open his eyes to the joy of his past Christmases, the opportunities he is missing in this one, and the unhappy end he faces if he keeps on his present isolated course. The next day, joyous that he can change the future by changing his behavior, he sends a prize turkey to the Cratchits, promises a large gift to the fund for the poor, goes to dinner at his nephew's, and generally enjoys himself hugely. Afterward, "it was always said of him, that he knew how to keep Christmas well, if any man alive possessed the knowledge."

Scrooge's Mistake

This lovely tale emphasizes a point about economic man that is of overriding importance to the spiritual case for liberty. That is, optimizing money income is quite a different thing from optimizing well-being. For all his profit motive, Scrooge before the ghosts' visits is not acting to "maximize his utility," in the economists' term. In his mania for money, he is a cold, loveless, bitter man. In economic terms again, the opportunity cost of his ceaseless accumulation of assets is the far greater wealth in "psychic income"—pleasure—that he forgoes. No doubt Scrooge is doing what he perceives to be in his self-interest—all of us are *homo economicus* to that extent—but as the ghosts show him, he is making catastrophic mistakes.

As he hears his nephew say, at Christmas dinner in the dream, "the consequence of his taking a dislike to us, and not making merry with us, is, I think, that he loses some pleasant moments, which could do him no harm. I am sure he loses pleasanter companions than he can find in his own thoughts, either in his mouldy old office, or his dusty chambers." Scrooge loses music, laughter, blind-man's buff and other games. He loses all sorts of things that, as he observes them by the Spirit's side, have tremendous appeal. His maniacal attention to money simply cannot be called self-interested.

The next day Scrooge leaves his ledgers behind for once and goes unexpectedly to his nephew's house. Christmas dinner transpires as he had seen it in the dream, except that now he participates: "Wonderful party, wonderful games, wonderful unanimity, wonderful happiness!" He has progressed from unhappiness to happiness in an evening, thanks to a change in focus from narrow money concerns alone to a broader concern that includes the rewards of positive human relationships.

A related point is that among the greatest psychic satisfactions available to human beings are those that come simply from doing something for others we care about. I would not be misunderstood here: I am not talking about any benefit to those we care for, but just about the benefit to ourselves—the happy satisfaction, the warm glow, the serene contentment for us—that comes as a result of benefiting others.

It is rather like a pure market exchange: there is benefit on both sides. Scrooge, newly concerned for the bravely struggling Cratchit family, gives them a prize turkey. They benefit thereby; indeed, they are probably transported with delight. But they don't benefit any more than Scrooge. For him the cost of the gift is only the price of the turkey, while the benefit to him, the psychic return in joy, is, well, let us get it exactly: "'I'll send it to Bob Cratchit's,' whispered Scrooge, rubbing his hands, and splitting with a laugh. . . . The chuckle with which he paid for the turkey, and the chuckle with which he paid for the cab, and the chuckle with which he recompensed the boy, were only to be exceeded by the chuckle with which he sat down breathless in his chair again, and chuckled till he cried."

Because others are important to us, it is in our own self-interest to give some attention to their well-being and, putting it impersonally, to invest in our relationships with them. These considerations apply beyond family and close acquaintances to the communities of which we are a part. Because we do live in our communities, community morale and standard of living have a bearing on our own quality of life. Hence it is self-interested to pay attention to the community and do what we reasonably can to improve it.

The Ghost of Christmas Present faces Scrooge with this in the persons of two children that cling to his robes:

> They were a boy and a girl. Yellow, meagre, ragged, scowling, wolfish; but prostrate, too, in their humility. . . . "They are man's," said the Spirit, looking down upon them. "And they cling to me, appealing from their fathers. This boy is Ignorance. This girl is Want. Beware of them both, and all of their degree. . . ." "Have they no refuge or resource?" cried Scrooge. "Are there no prisons!" said the Spirit. . . . "Are there no workhouses?"

Here we must be careful to grant the validity of Dickens' point without guessing at his policy prescriptions. Experience with the Poor Law in his time, as well as many years of experience with the modern welfare state, show how very difficult it is to help poor people. Often the effort to do so, especially in a bureaucratic structure that operates by rule rather than by judgment about individual needs, creates disincentives to self-help, and thereby perpetuates poverty. The workhouses which Dickens hates were a government effort to care for the poor. The best we can do for such unhappy souls may well be not to give them much, but rather to work for the repeal of bad laws which obstruct their advancement. In any case, the point remains that since our lives and fortunes are tied up with theirs, it is in our self-interest to do what we may to improve their quality of life. Charity can be at once generous and self-interested.

The Importance of Spiritual Goods

Another lesson of "A Christmas Carol" that can fortify the spiritual case for liberty is that material goods are often a prerequisite for spiritual goods. We tend sometimes to think that there is an either/or choice among these, too. Either we concern ourselves with "higher" matters of love, community, and doing well by others (good!), or we concern ourselves with the "low" business of producing and accumulating physical stuff (bad!).

But we are creatures of flesh and blood as well as of spirit, and we must be fed, clothed, and sheltered adequately if the spirit is to soar. We can do little for others or ourselves if we lack the means to do it with. And ultimately all money—indeed, all material goods—are means to spiritual or psychic ends. We don't want them for themselves, but for the satisfactions they can give. Scrooge discovers during the ghosts' visits that his piles of wealth are valueless to him if all he ever does is pile up more. Not until he uses his money does he "cash in" on the psychic satisfactions that are the point of the whole endeavor.

Consider the story's final episode, when Scrooge reveals his changed self to Cratchit. He says earnestly,

> "A merry Christmas, Bob! . . . A merrier Christmas, Bob, my good fellow, than I have given you for many a year! I'll raise your salary, and endeavor to assist your

struggling family, and we will discuss your affairs this very afternoon, over a Christmas bowl of smoking bishop, Bob! Make up the fires, and buy another coal scuttle before you dot another i, Bob Cratchit!"

Good for generous Scrooge! His attention now encompasses the "higher matter" of his clerk's well-being. (By the way, observes the economist, Cratchit's productivity will probably increase substantially.) But how could Scrooge be generous without his cash? What would pay the higher salary, go to assist the family, buy the Christmas bowl and extra coal? Praise the Lord for Scrooge's money and his ability to earn it! May he continue to do so! It's cash that lets a generous impulse become a generous deed.

Now of course I don't mean to imply that in a free economy all will realize the extent to which their happiness increases by generous concern for others. Certainly in a free society some people will choose a low, selfish, small-spirited, narrow way of life. Surely they will be less happy because of this choice than they would otherwise be. And not all of them will have Scrooge's good luck in being brought back to his senses by the intervention of kindly Spirits of some kind. This is to be lamented.

But this unfortunate choice of a less happy rather than a more happy way of life is just that—a choice. It is not caused by the free society which allows it; it is caused by the individual's own short-sightedness, unwisdom, and inability to perceive that real self-interest depends substantially on other-regarding activities.

The good life involves a judicious balance of self- and other-regarding activities. When the balance is a healthy one, these two reinforce each other and merge. The wonderful thing about the free society is that it allows human beings such broad scope in which to pursue and fulfill all their values, whatever they may be—material, personal, spiritual—and puts in our way an abundance of resources and opportunities with which to pursue them all.

An afterthought: one aspect of "A Christmas Carol" that bears mention is that the ghosts work by persuasion. They do not take Scrooge's money and hand it over to the Cratchits (Bob Cratchit would likely have refused it on that basis anyway). They simply present to Scrooge the truth and let him decide for himself what he will do about it, if anything. They confront him with reality, but respect his liberty and property. (It makes one wonder if Dickens himself would have approved of the transfer taxation of the welfare state.)

That is the admirable, respectful way to influence people's ideas and behavior—to enlighten and to persuade. That has been Paul L. Poirot's manner and accomplishment for more years than I can account for. He has exemplified the balance discussed here, working hard at a job less remunerative than many he might have held, in service of principles and a cause he cares about. In pursuing his self-interest as he saw it, he has enriched us all. Thanks, Paul. Merry Christmas. And "God bless us, every one!"

Mr. Baetjer, a former member of the staff at FEE, is currently a doctoral student at George Mason University in Fairfax, Virginia.

Fair Pricing:
The Persistent Delusion

BY MELVIN D. BARGER

ONE of the most durable delusions of our time is that there should be a "fair" price for everything. We hear this expressed in a number of ways. If prices are too low, it's ruinous and the producers are being sacrificed to the gods of chance. But if prices are too high, the situation is exploitative and the sellers are gouging the public. In either case, the solution offered is the same: A public authority should rescue the producers when prices are too low and rein in the sellers when prices are too high. All this is for the public good, it's argued, and we're all supposed to receive indirect benefits if "fair" prices bail out the producers or restrain the sellers.

This sounds like a fine solution, since none of us likes being ruined or gouged. In practice, though, it has been destructive in every way it has been tried. It fails, many of us think, because values really are established *subjectively*. It is misleading to call prices unfair because they are considered "too low" or "too high." Prices in themselves are only market expressions of *subjective value*—in much the same way as thermometer readings express the weather temperature.

The strange thing about subjective value is that almost every economics textbook used in the United States tacitly accepts it as true—yet some also try to evade it by defending interventions aimed at establishing price supports and controls. When this results in long-run failures, few economists are willing to admit that the basic error was in ignoring subjective value.

What is subjective value? Here's a definition supplied by Bettina Bien Greaves, a long-time staff member of The Foundation for Economic Education. "Subjective value is basic to the Austrian School of Economics," Mrs. Greaves explains. "It wraps up the Austrian point of view, and everything else follows from it. Subjective value means that every individual has a personal scale of values. By acting on those values, the individual directs production, determines prices, decides who is to make profits or suffer losses, determines what commodity is most marketable, and even decides what is money."[1]

There are other theories of value. One theory is that certain things have *intrinsic* value. Another is the *labor* theory, which tries to establish values by the labor required for production. Neither theory can be supported by the behavior of the market. Intrinsic value? Nothing really has a set value in and of itself. Even commodities like gold, which always seem to fetch some kind of a price, are valued differently at different times and in different places. The labor theory? Almost anybody should be able to disprove the labor theory, since we all have labored at times on things that proved to be worthless in the current market! Even Karl Marx recognized this. "Nothing can have value without being an object of utility," he said in *Capital.* "If it be useless, the labor contained in it is useless, cannot be reckoned as labor, and cannot therefore create value."[2]

It's interesting that "utility" pops out in Marx's statement, since subjective value is also called marginal utility. What it really means is that our values cause us to put our individual resources to different uses. Eugen von Böhm-Bawerk, a founder (with Carl Menger) of Austrian economics, used the example of a pioneer farmer in the jungle of Brazil: The farmer has just harvested five sacks of grain. One he needs simply to stay alive at the subsistence level. The second sack will assure him of a *full* diet, while the third will feed his poultry and thus provide him with meat. Finally, he uses the fourth sack to make brandy and the fifth to feed his pet parrots.[3]

There's a scale of values at work here. The first sack is obviously very dear, since it stands between the farmer and dying. Most farmers might value the first three sacks in the same way, while choosing to use sacks four and five in alternate ways. The point of this illustration is that each of us is the Brazilian farmer and our available resources (usually money) are the sacks of grain. We put our resources out to market in the hope of meeting certain needs on our scale of values. As individuals, we each want to get the most satisfaction with the least expenditure of resources. Prices reflect the ways thousands of people are trying to satisfy their wants and needs in the market. If we use only peaceful methods, each of us can satisfy individual wants and needs only by supplying something valued by others. The economics textbooks use supply and demand curves to illustrate how this process works, and the "equilibrium price" is always the level that balances the determinants of both demand and supply.

In these graphs, "too low" or "too high" does not come into play. The point is made, however, that if prices are kept above the equilibrium level (say, with price supports), then excessive production occurs. On the other hand, if prices are held down (say, with price controls), excessive consumption occurs. It could easily be shown that this causes harm by distorting production and consumption patterns, but it shouldn't be necessary to make this point.

Are Low Prices Ruinous?

Subjective value, being individual, cannot include any overall judgment that condemns any price level as too low. Certain individuals may feel, of course, that a specific price level is too low and therefore unfair to their own group of producers. Since they may feel it is in their own interests to raise prices above what the market will give them, they seek special legislation to boost or support their prices. This legislation would be turned back if others realized that the price increases would be at their expense. To win passage of such legislation, it is necessary to convey the idea that the change is in the public interest—that we all benefit if these prices are raised.

Rather than be angered by this, we have to remember that subjective value explains why groups will seek special advantage through legislation. They do so in the hope of getting more at less cost to themselves. When they seem to succeed in this effort, it is useless to condemn them as being greedy and selfish. Instead, we should ask why we permitted them to deceive us.

Farmers and some blue-collar workers have been the most successful in winning support for their price interests. Beginning in the 1930s, farmers were able to delude the public into believing that higher farm prices would restore prosperity! In the same period, workers were able to get minimum wage laws passed and protective labor legislation which enabled them to raise their wages (i.e., the prices of their services). The public was led to believe that low farm prices hurt everybody and that workers needed legislation and Federally guaranteed union protection in order to rise above a barely living wage. It was a case of defending the farmer from predatory "middlemen" who took all the profits and shielding the laborer from heartless employers who were only one step removed from Ebenezer Scrooge.

All this was nonsense. Though farm prices were low in the 1930s, they were not ruinously so and some farmers knew how to operate profitably during that bleak period. You could also prove, by studying the food processing and distribution system, that there were no middlemen reaping huge profits at the farmers' expense. Everybody in the system, from grain broker to miller to baker to grocer, was struggling to stay solvent. Drought and pestilence were really the things to worry about in some parts of the Midwest. A low price, far from being ruinous, is simply a signal the market is sending. It should either help direct production into new commodity lines or force some farmers out of business, with the land being taken over by others who can use it more efficiently.

It's not even true that all farmers resent low prices at all times. A farmer who buys corn to feed cattle, for example, might like lower corn prices. This can eventually result in lower beef prices for the consumer, something most of us might welcome.

What about the "slave" wages that are supposedly paid to workers if there is no intervention? The low wages of the Depression were actually helping to return some people to work following the terrible dislocations of the Great Crash. Unemployment was severe in the high-wage industries like auto manufacturing and steelmaking, less so in lower wage businesses like food processing. Though low wages were seen as ruinous to some employees, anything that mandated higher wages might have been more ruinous in the sense of putting them out of work. The wage level was not dictated by Scrooge-like employers. Faithful to subjective value, it reported the signals from consumers. The worker who complained about his own ruinously low wages, for example, was also determining by his purchases the price levels and activities in other businesses.

The truth is, low prices are neither good nor bad in a free market. They are merely signals which tell us how to direct production and consumption. What's really bad is anything that distorts those signals in such a way that we can no longer make the right spending and investment decisions. Efforts to support prices and maintain wages at certain levels have set in motion endless mischief which has not been corrected.

One last thought: Subjective value being what it is, all of us are simply delighted when we find a sensational markdown at a department store or catch the supermarket when it has to sell an overstock of perishable produce at below cost. We do not think we are taking advantage of these retailers, and in truth we are not. By helping ourselves, we also help them avoid total losses for bad purchasing decisions. Are we not also helping the farmer or the laborer by paying market-clearing prices for their commodities and services? Is it somehow better if the farmer is "priced out of the market" or the wage level is raised so that the worker becomes unemployed?

Are High Prices a Form of Gouging?

The same zeal that condemns low prices can often be found when prices seem inordinately high. The villains are often the "speculators"—people who have bought up certain supplies in the hope of making a later profit. In American folklore, the speculator is always a person who is up to no good. Speculators sometimes get the blame for high prices when in fact they have merely been extremely shrewd in estimating price trends.

High prices, no less than low ones, can be explained by subjective value. They are signals which should help direct production for those who can read them. In manufacturing, prices help guide innovation and progress. That's because competition and other forces tend to drive prices down, thus squeezing earnings on older product lines. This forces business people to branch out into new products which fetch a higher price. Without the opportunity to seek that higher price (with its higher earnings), no business would want to risk the required investment or even take the trouble to innovate.

Consumers need not fret about the high price tags new products carry at introduction. If free market conditions prevail, the high prices will not last—competitors quickly join the race and fight for market share. This cycle has occurred so frequently with new products that the public can even recognize it. It's not a surprise to anybody, for example, that the prices of video tape recorders tumbled recently. This happened previously to a wide range of products: TV sets, riding mowers, microwave ovens—you name it.

Despite these clear examples, there's still a suspicion that high prices will hurt us. In wartime, for example, there's an immediate rush to price controls. When the oil shortage hit, there was a cap on producer prices. We've also seen demands for controls on doctors' fees. Rent control still survives in New York City, even though it is obviously a failure.

Far from trying to punish and control the so-called price gougers, we should stand back and read the message of the high prices. These high prices are more of a blessing than we think. In a wartime situation, high prices immediately spur people to reduce consumption and to hunt for low-cost substitutes. If there is an oil and gas shortage, higher prices encourage conservation, new drilling and exploration and the hunt for substitute energy. If rents are high, more apartment buildings will be constructed, eventually creating a glut that will bring some rents down. As for doctors' fees, they've been unduly distorted by third-party payments and other special demand factors. A genuine free market in health care services would do wonders in bringing prices down.

The point of all this is that there is no such thing as real price gouging in a free market. We need the signals of high prices.

A final note: For a time after World War II, the government kept the prices of new automobiles artificially low, though used cars were allowed to sell at market-determined prices. This created a ridiculous situation: A new car would sell for $1,300 at the dealership and immediately would become worth $2,600 as a used car! Needless to say, some dealers responded to this distorted situation by accepting money under the table or by demanding a used-car trade-in at a low price. Along with used-car dealers, they were denounced as price gougers.

The strange thing, however, is that everybody was a price gouger. Anybody who had a car for sale automatically wanted the higher price, not the low one deemed "fair" by the government. Well, why not? We all want to sell high and buy low—that's well understood by the students of subjective value.

Understanding Value—A Key to Fairness

Despite all the evidence against it, the arguments for "fair" prices are likely to continue. These arguments will still sell in the political arena when they're framed in appealing ways. Farm price supports and wage legislation had political support because the farmer and blue-collar worker represented large groups and were cast as underdogs. In the same way, there are times when you can win support for price controls aimed at unpopular groups: doctors, the large auto companies, and so on.

In our personal economic decisions, however, we continue to be guided by our own scales of values. We may pity the farmer and wish him well, but we are stern taskmasters who look for bargains when we buy farm products. We may sympathize with the blue-collar worker, but if his wages force the employer to raise prices, we shift to another supplier without shedding a tear.

In the same way, we denounce high prices but always determine the going market price when we want to make a sale. If real estate prices double in our area, for example, none of us hesitates for a moment in making a windfall profit when the time comes to sell a home. We don't even think it unfair that the new homeowners have to pay twice the price we once paid!

If there is unfairness, it's not in "too low" or "too high" prices. It's in misguided efforts that distort the price signals that will really work for our good in the long run. Nobody can really say what a "fair" price is—but we can say with certainty that the price of self-deception about pricing is always high.

Mr. Barger, a retired corporate public relations representative, is now a writer-consultant in Toledo, Ohio.

---

1. Obtained by author in telephone discussion with Mrs. Greaves in early 1976. Statement has been slightly modified for this article. The Austrian School, also called free-market economics, got its name because its prominent teachers, Böhm-Bawerk and Menger, were Austrian. Ludwig von Mises and Friedrich A. Hayek are also identified with Austrian economics.

2. Cited in *Familiar Quotations*, by John Bartlett, Little, Brown and Company, Boston, Thirteenth Edition, 1955, p. 593.

3. *Value and Price*, Eugen von Böhm-Bawerk, Libertarian Press, South Holland, Ill., published in 1973 from earlier work, pp. 29–30.

The Right to Property

BY CLARENCE B. CARSON

AT our house, we have a cat who sometimes goes by the name of Felix, a rather scrawny but well-fed black male with some white markings. His turf has been persistently trespassed upon by our next-door neighbor's male cat, a solid black furry animal who is called Leo. We suspect that Leo has his application in to become our cat, because he acts as if he owns the deck at the back of our house. Felix has always viewed this interloping askance, but for a good while he evaded the issue by going in and out the front doors. He was clearly becoming increasingly disturbed by Leo's intrusion, however, because instances in which he hissed, growled, and made guttural sounds of his displeasure were becoming more numerous. Then, one morning he apparently decided he had had more than enough of Leo's impertinence. He went about the periphery of our lot marking off his territory in a manner peculiar to four-legged animals, or at least cats and dogs. Having clearly marked the boundaries, Felix then jumped the trespasser, chased him into his own yard, and drove him up a tree. As if to warn him against further trespass, he lay under the tree until wearying of the assignment, daring Leo to come down.

Many animals protect their particular turf from intruders by primal instinct, whether it be cats fighting with other cats, bees defending their hives from those who would rob them of their honey, ants protecting their beds, or what not. This sense of some animals having a turf which they protect has been dubbed the "territorial imperative." It is akin to man's claim to real property in land based upon occupancy or homesteading. Indeed, states generally recognize claims to land by occupants after they have asserted that claim for a period of years without challenge.

Small children develop very early a sense of certain objects being theirs. Undoubtedly, they have a much stronger awareness of "mine" than "thine," for they tend to have little compunction picking up and playing with another child's toy, but assert vigorously the claim to their own.

These facts, and others that could be cited, suggest that the right to property is deeply rooted in our nature, and that we even share some of its basic aspects with the lower animals. Although the right to property can be rationally explained and justified, there is good reason to believe that the determination to have and assert such a right is prerational in origin. It stems from the most basic aspect of all life, the determination to survive, mature, and achieve that form implanted in us. It derives from that instinct which presses the plant to bend toward the sunlight when it is deprived, that sends the roots of trees deep into the ground, that causes the dog to bury a bone, that pushes the ant to store up bits of food in season, that fuels the quest for sustenance by man and his willingness to defend his store of it ferociously. It is of the will to survive.

Property Rights vs. "Human Rights"

Intellectuals—socialist casuists mainly—have made the argument in this century that the right to property is, if it exists at all, an inferior right. It is inferior, they say, to what they are pleased to call "human rights." It is inferior, they say more specifically, to freedom of speech, freedom of religion, freedom of assembly, and the like. However valuable and important these rights are—and they are important and valuable—those who argue in this fashion have got the matter wrong end to. Far from being inferior to them, the right to property is the most basic of all rights. Without the individual's right to property none of these other rights can subsist. The right to property is foundational. It is the mother, so to speak, of all other rights. The superiority of the right to property resides in the nature of things.

Look at it this way. Which right is essential to survival? To growth and development? To the achievement of maturity? Is freedom of speech, for example, essential to survival? Of course, it is not. On the contrary, it is quite possible to survive, as many people have, without even encountering the notion of free speech. The same is true for freedom of the press, the right to peaceful assembly, and even the alleged "right" to vote. Nor are they really essential to growth and development or the achieving of maturity, though they would be quite helpful to some people, at least.

Property is in a category all by itself, in regard to these basics of life. Survival is impossible without the use of property in land. Such property provides us the very space for living on earth. Without it, we have no place to walk, eat, sleep, stand, breathe, drink, work, or even to be. The plant life so necessary to our survival in providing food, fiber, and wood is rooted in the land. Nor, given some place to stand and be, could we survive without property rights in the food, clothing, houses, and tools that we use. Nor could we grow and develop without a property in the means for doing so. As for maturity and fulfillment, these could not be unless we survived, grew, and developed. Without some sort of property rights, if we were to survive at all, it could only be as the slaves or servants of those who held the property.

Property rights, it should be emphasized, entail much more that the right to land and the fixtures upon it. Property rights extend to every species of property, to anything that can be justly owned by a person: all that we have produced with our hands and tools from our materials, or portions thereof, or acquired from others by voluntary exchange. There is a notion that has been around for quite some while, too, that it would be possible for property to be held in common—as in primitive communism, for example. If we look at the notion closely, we will see that it is ultimately an illusion. Property must ultimately be used or consumed by persons as individuals, whether it is a car to be driven or a piece of cake to be eaten. At that point, its commonality must cease, if not well before. The right to property, then, with some familiar exceptions, is ultimately the right to private property in the control and use of something. The above discussion has been made mainly for the purpose of establishing the essentiality of property to life. Thus, I have not gone at all into the diverse and complex ways that property and its rights may be parceled out, divided, alienated or held. In any case, that would be a topic requiring something much nearer to a volume for adequate treatment than an essay.

Nor is it my intent to downgrade such rights as free speech and a free press. They are no less rights because they are rights derived from property rights. Free speech is derived from the property one has in his own person. This property right translates mainly into the right to control and use one's own faculties for his own ends. Undoubtedly, this right may be restricted so as, for example, to use them constructively not destructively, but it is nonetheless, by derivation, a property right. If a person does not have the right to the constructive use of his faculties for his own end, he is a slave of someone else, whose property he is. Speech is a faculty, and freedom of speech is merely an affirmation of the right to use that faculty constructively.

Freedom of the press clearly derives from the use of property, namely, a printing press. Moreover, it is a freedom which can only be exercised at the behest or by the person who owns or controls a press. The right to constructive use of a press is a right such as was understood to pertain to the use of all property in the United States. Undoubtedly, speech, press, religion, and assembly received mention in the Constitution because they were matters upon which governments had shown a penchant for restricting in times past. Most likely, if governments had shown a like inclination in earlier times to restrict the use of grist mills, saw mills, or plows, the Constitution might have established a freedom of grist milling, saw milling, and plowing. Of course, they never dreamed that those who governed would be likely to concern themselves with such mundane affairs.

19

Thoughtful men were well aware at the time of the making of the Constitution, that it would be a forbidding, if not impossible, task to list all the particular rights that comprehend liberty and property. Bills of rights usually covered only those that had been in doubt in times past. Thus, the Constitution does not even list the rights of property ownership, such as the rights to hold, to divide, to use for your own benefit, to dispose, and to sell or otherwise alienate yourself from it. The rights of property, in any extension, were just assumed.

Yet, the right to property was recognized in the United States Constitution, and in state constitutions in most cases. It was understood as a *natural* right, not as a governmentally granted privilege. The greatest assault on property rights in the past century has come from socialists. But they have been greatly assisted in the discrediting of property rights by proponents of *Realpolitik,* or the modern Machiavellians, those who see things purely in terms of government power. These latter generally argue that all so-called rights are really grants of government. While there should be no doubt that government may intrude upon or deny rights, it does not follow that it is *right* in doing so, or that it has the right to do so. Such a political view simply denies the existence of rights.

It is socialist ideas, however, that have provided the cutting edge in the assault on property in this century. Socialists have from the outset denied that individuals have legitimate or just claims to property, or to rights in it. They have tended to see private property, especially in land and in the alleged means of production, as special privileges granted and protected by government. While socialist thought has hardly followed one consistent line, they have held that productive property is, was, or should be commonly owned. Without some power to make continual allocations, the notion is no more than a will-of-the-wisp, since it is not possible to utilize or consume property without someone controlling it to the exclusion of all other claims upon it. Try, for example, to eat a grape or to plow with a tractor in common. In practice, socialists are bent on vesting the power of allocation in government, although gradualists move toward that goal with many subterfuges.

Property Is a Natural Right

It is not my purpose here, however, to make a utilitarian or pragmatic argument for private property. On the contrary, my point is not only that property is a natural right but also that this is the surest defense of it. As an intellectual exercise, utilitarians and even pragmatists may make an interesting defense of private property. If tom cats could reason, they might make a good case that each one of them should stick to his own territory and not intrude upon the other. But as matters stand, tom cats do instinctively what men must be prepared to do ultimately in defense of what is presumptively theirs. Men must defend their property as theirs by right, for if they have a just claim, it is just that. Anything less will not do.

The burden of this essay has been to show that property is a right, that it is a right antecedent to government, to constitutions, to institutions, or to any organization of society. It is derived from the nature of man and of life on earth, a right coterminous with the right to exist. We must have property to exist, and the surest foundation of that is in property as a right. That is not to say that it is some sort of birthright to be accorded some particular property, or that we have a right to the property. On the contrary, the right to property extends only to that property we have earned, bought, or that has been given to us. It is at that point that the right to property comes into play. Nor is it my intent to deny that property may be properly taxed by government. But if the right to property is to be maintained, taxation must be limited in ways to keep it from ever being confiscatory, for then the right to property tends to be nullified.

In any case, the best defense and ultimately claim to property is that it is held by right. The best example that comes to mind of this truth concerns the historic claim of Americans to gold. When Franklin D. Roosevelt came to the presidency, a great many Americans owned either gold or currency and other notes redeemable in gold. The New Deal called in all gold and eventually nullified all promises to pay in gold. That gold and the promises to pay was the property of Americans. It was theirs by right. Once they had turned it in, they lost all claim upon that property. No great loss was immediately apparent, at least not in purchasing power of the medium of exchange. The Federal Reserve notes and silver certificates which replaced the gold would exchange for as much as the gold—over the short run. Americans were assured that their currency was still backed by gold, and the legend that Federal Reserve notes bore in those days indicated that they were redeemable in lawful money. But, of course, they could only be redeemed in silver or Federal Reserve notes. The stage was set for what did indeed happen, a long-term and ongoing inflation which moves in the direction of the ultimate destruction of the money. There was only one point in time and one position on which it could have been stopped with no loss or confiscation: when it was called in and on the basis that the gold belonged to the owners by right. Whatever opportunity there was to succeed at that was lost, largely by default.

Dr. Clarence B. Carson has written and taught extensively, specializing in American intellectual history. He is the author of the recently published Basic History of the United States, *a five-volume text.*

"Fabianism-In-Reverse"

BY JOHN CHAMBERLAIN

IN THE late Forties and early Fifties a lot of things happened to challenge the dominant belief in collectivism. Leonard Read, coming East from California, started The Foundation for Economic Education, familiarly known as FEE. Friedrich Hayek, the Austrian economist, and a chosen group of old-fashioned classical liberals met on a mountain top in Switzerland to found the Mont Pelerin Society. The *Freeman* magazine, reviving a name that recalled the libertarianism of Albert Jay Nock in the Twenties, began publication, helped by Alfred Kohlberg's willing switch of money he had been giving to sustain Don Levine's *Plain Talk*, an excellent magazine that had made common cause with socialists in opposing the Stalinism of the times.

It was with some difficulty that Henry Hazlitt, Suzanne LaFollette and I, as the first *Freeman* editors, assembled eight pertinent articles for a first issue. The aim was to support the true liberal position as well as to fight what was happening in Russia. Once our flag was unfurled, with the faith of *The Freeman* succinctly stated by Henry Hazlitt, the articles began to flow. Robert Morris, minority counselor of the Tydings Subcommittee in Washington, reported on the testimony of various individuals who had had a hand in shaping our disastrous China policy. Ludwig von Mises contributed an illuminating essay on Lord Keynes and Say's Law. And Frank Chodorov, in a sardonic defense of the bookmaker's function in the gambling world, observed for us that human nature simply refused to be collectivized.

Chodorov, who delivered his articles and reviews in person, was both amused by and tolerant of our gung-ho expectations. He told us we were going to win, but it would take more than twenty years to do it. He reminded us of the history of the Fabian Society in England. What we must do, he said, was to invoke a Fabianism-in-reverse. The "inevitability of gradualism" that had led to British socialism must be turned in an opposite direction. And so it was. But it took time and persistence even to build to the exciting Goldwater year of 1964, which made the later triumph of Ronald Reagan possible.

Frank Chodorov was himself the editor of *The Freeman* for a brief period before it was turned into a monthly purveyor of "ideas on liberty" for FEE. He gave way to failing health, but not without getting in some trenchant last licks before handing over the editorial pencil to Paul Poirot. Meanwhile Willi Schlamm, who had been Henry Luce's war-time adviser on European affairs, had persuaded Bill Buckley to start *National Review*. Bill had just written his *God and Man at Yale*.

It was Fabianism-in-reverse for Bill Buckley to mount the first attack on an entrenched Keynesian economics faculty at an Ivy League University. He couldn't hope to win all at once by commanding history to stop. Paul Samuelson, perhaps the leading American economist of the time, was already riding high when Frank Chodorov was warning us to get ready for a twenty-year battle. Samuelson's textbook advocating Keynesian fine-tuning to keep the economy on an even keel was being adopted in elementary economics courses everywhere. John Kenneth Galbraith predicted that a whole generation would get their economics from Samuelson. It was a good prediction but, ironically, it was Samuelson's own vulnerability to events that was to undermine the bright Keynesian confidence of the early editions of his text.

Year by year Samuelson was to lower the limits of a permissive rate of inflation. The changes in twelve successive editions of Samuelson have been ably charted by Burton Yale Pines in his *Back to Basics* and by Professor Thomas J. DiLorenzo in a notable article in the Heritage Foundation's *Policy Review*. Little by little, as the reverse Fabians have had at him, Samuelson has surrendered his certainties. The culminating irony, as DiLorenzo has noted, is the endorsement by Samuelson (and his Yale collaborator William D. Nordhaus) of the theory of public choice. This theory insists that political supporters of "planning," or of monetary and fiscal intervention, have their own career decisions to consider. They are by no means disinterested guardians of the general welfare. Because of this, as Samuelson now says, "we must be alert to *government failure*—situations in which governments cause diseases or make them worse." (The telltale italics are Samuelson's own.)

Samuelson now asserts that "politics, like the market, has its framework and its players." Who are the players? They include consumers who have the vote. But the "other major players examined in public choice theory are the elected representatives, or politicians. This group performs a function much like that of firms in a market economy—they match up tastes and technology. They interpret the public's demand for collective goods and find ways of supplying these goods."

The Entitlement Game

Samuelson now asks what drives politicians? A few will risk defeat on issues that they care about deeply. A few would rather be right than be president. But it is a reasonable assumption that most of them "behave so as to maximize their chances of reelection . . . they are assumed to be vote maximizers—just as firms are taken to be profit maximizers."

Vote maximizing leads to logrolling, horsetrading and all the manifestations of political "pork." The game of entitlements is played without any regard for the overall budget. In default of a gold standard to impose limitations on the money issue to pay for entitlements, inflation is the end result. It can come, as Howard Ruff has indicated, in malarial spurts.

Samuelson recognizes all of this now. The ironic thing is that his opinions are a distinct echo of what Nobel Prize winner James M. Buchanan, the foremost partisan of the public choice theory, has been telling his non-Keynesian colleagues. Buchanan has just completed a term as President of the Mont Pelerin Society. The Buchanan echo mingles with that of Milton Friedman, another Mont Pelerin president and Nobel Prize winner in economics.

To be sure, Samuelson might say that his lucid paraphrasing of public choice doctrine does not wholly commit himself or his collaborator, Nordhaus, to it. But his admission that Keynesian fine-tuning can result in government failure is what is new under the Samuelson sun.

It is also new to witness Samuelson's concern for the Federal deficit, which according to the latest Consumers' Alert figures, stands at $221 billion. "We need to stop the bleeding," says Buchanan, "stop eating up what belongs to future generations. We're literally eating up goods and services through our public sector that taxpayers in future periods are going to have to pay for."

Samuelson now talks about government programs that, once begun, "take on a charmed existence . . . governments often behave like the little boy who said, 'I know how to spell bananas, but I don't know when to stop.'"

With the colleges turning to free market texts (an Alchian-Allen text is having a good run), and with Samuelson himself now criticizing those who are "nonchalant about inflation," Frank Chodorov's predictions are certainly being borne out. Twenty and more years of Fabianism-in-reverse have significantly altered the political and economic climate.

Alas, our logrolling lobbies haven't yet caught the pitch. They are still attempting to function as they have always functioned. Witness the drive for protectionism. But they are now getting something of a comeuppance. Almost every week in Washington brings news of the doings of what might be called the "anti-lobby lobby." We have the new conservative think tanks such as Ed Feulner's Heritage Foundation and the American Enterprise Institute. We have the Citizens for a Sound Economy and the Cato Institute. We have the Washington offshoot of the London Adam Smith Institute.

With good watchdogs on Capitol Hill the anti-lobby lobbies are in a position to forestall the more egregious "vote maximizers." Frank Chodorov would have been amused to observe that Paul Samuelson has done something to bring this about.

As a critic, a journalist, and an editor of such periodicals as Fortune, Harper's, *and* National Review, *John Chamberlain is regarded as one of America's most distinguished men of letters.*

Individualism Revisited: A Castle in the Clouds

by Ridgway K. Foley, Jr.

ACCORDING to G. K. Chesterton, "There are no rules of architecture for a castle in the clouds." Substantial similarity exists between the eminent Mr. Chesterton and my redoubtable friend and mentor Paul Poirot. Each man qualifies as a remarkable wordsmith; each demonstrates eclectic knowledge; each operates on high principle. Thus, it seems fitting to employ a Chesterton epigram in tribute to Paul Poirot.

Chesterton's trenchant observation reminds us that the glory of individual action lies in its very lack of prescribed form and fetters. Of course, nature provides some constraints: We would not do at all well in a random universe. However, avoidance of artificial barriers allows full sway to man to construct his "castle in the clouds," to permit his mind to expand, develop, and search for a destiny beyond the ken of a coercive committee.

In essence, one must choose between contract and coercion. A contractual society exists upon the premise that men can arrange their affairs voluntarily and with good faith; that persons seeking their self-interest can better plan and provide for a desired outcome than can the omnipotent state; that endless variations require specific treatment impossible under the strictures of general codes; and, that a moral order pervades the universe. The statist society leaves precious little room for the grace of individualism—the puny minds of legislators and bureaucrats seek to foreordain all possible outcomes by virtue of prior restraints they concoct. The result: a dull, faceless, and tasteless society, to say the least.

A contractual society requires law—rules of societal architecture, if you will—only to solve otherwise insoluble disputes and to thwart aggression; it allows the contracting parties, absent force and fraud, to preordain their ends. Contrast the prevailing view: "Modern political leaders reject the importance of private contracts; government rules are written for everything. Individual rights are never defended; special class 'rights' (which are actually demands and wishes) are used as guidelines."[1]

Contrary to the prevailing political mode, one ought to be concerned with the dignity, the worth, and the sanctity of the individual human being. Each individual is unique, and this unique quality, this discrete difference, is the source from which all values flow. This difference in values produces the need to engage in exchange, to trade peacefully, and to form those voluntary associations which satisfy human needs for companionship and security, for civility and development. Those who decry individual action seek regulation in all important matters of human existence. Regulation implies the need for coercive control; it preordains the ultimate demise of individualism.

The Dogma of Creeds

Why does society[2] impose controls which inevitably stifle creativity and inhibit advance? Regulation affords an acceptable label to camouflage coercive restraint of free, creative human conduct which, if unchained, might dispatch wonderful energy and miraculous results for the individual or mankind or both. Codes, no matter what their origin and their well-intended meaning, are always shortsighted because the draftsmen (being fellows of wee minds) cannot foresee the developments which will flow from the unchanneled conduct of millions upon millions of discrete, contemplative individuals. Codes are always rigid and inflexible, geared to the lowest common denominator. Codifiers lack foresight and insight; their castles crumble, so they assault their neighbor's citadel, armed with law books and envy. Policing ultimately implies force; it forms the first step to a totalitarian state. It also implies sameness, limits upon creativity, and dullness.

Current emphasis upon societal rights and individual obligations does more than blur fundamental distinctions: It skews accurate analysis. "Class" or "societal" rights represent an impossibility: No aggregate possesses rights; rights belong to individuals, merely because they are individuals; rights do not inhere in mobs, in associations, or in claques. Indeed, since decisions emanate from personal individual choice, aggregate analysis is unhelpful. The unique characteristic of man as man, as distinct from all other creatures, is his capacity for moral choice. Man possesses the potential for evil as well as for good, and therein lies his humanity. Although man may be influenced by his heredity and by his environment, he is not fully determined by those forces: In essence, man is moral choice.[3]

Despite this seminal trait ineluctably present in mankind, we live, more and more, in an age of enforced orthodoxy. Lip service to liberty tumbles before the narrow constraints of a prescribed agenda. Punishment for thought or action beyond narrow "acceptable" limits exceeds the mere excommunication prevalent in earlier times: it may partake of compelled participation, imprisonment, torture, or death. While enforced orthodoxy was ever thus, the current situation differs radically from the past: the modern mandate state reigns during a period of rhapsodic lip service to tenets of liberty, tolerance, and pluralism. In simple terms, cant and hypocrisy mar the day: freedom for all who cleave to the prescribed agenda; the rack for those deserving wretches who deign to think the unthinkable, who seek heaven beyond the boundaries so carefully circumscribed by the legislators of the mind.

Extending One's Vision

Individualism, in its pure sense, recognizes the inherent, unlimited right to create one's "castle in the clouds" *sans* adherence to any scholastic governor, without sanction for heresy or apostasy. Properly construed, the philosophy of the volunteer, of the individualist, comprises the most tolerant of all human conditions: Absent aggressive and deceitful conduct, each individual enjoys the inherent right and power to extend his vision to the heights and depths of his desires. The open texture of individual action flows spontaneously, without preconceived ends: The majority may consider the dreamer foolish, wasteful, or goofy, but his quest remains unhindered.

Individualism is not egoism in its brittle and distasteful sense. Mankind seems bent on theocratic imposition, and few are immune from the virus of swell-headed certainty. The old theocratic society, oft characterized by blue laws and cant, sought to impose upon the social order a particular view of morality and good behavior. The new theocracies, although not so identified, also seek to conform all human behavior to a compulsive norm wherein the state or its minions define "good works" in the socialist tongue and impose their rules quite as arbitrarily as their precursors. Thus, the bigots of yore forbade bawdy houses and demon rum, whilst the illiberal moderns snub South Africa and Robert Bork, and preclude rational discourse by their opponents concerning legitimate religious, political, and moral controversies. Not to be outdone, the rationalist of the day—particularly in the political spectrum—reads out of his doctrinaire splinter movement those who seek to argue, e.g., concerning the issue of abortion or the precept of a limited government. Just so, the assault on judicial activism of the Warren years takes on quite a different hue with the elevation of "conservative" social engineers to the high court. All theocracies, old and new, overt and covert, partake of the same listless error: the cocksure belief in personal infallibility concurrent with a demeaning disregard for those who disagree.

Return to the lesson of Chesterton's phrase: "There are no rules of architecture for a castle in the clouds." Shackles deprive us all. Limiting rules inhibit advance and condemn us to a stagnant past. Committee action reduces contemplation to the peat bogs of the mind. Useless regulations provide but illusive certainty in an uncertain life. Free individual action, far from lacking order, provides the most orderly and felicitous fulfillment of the human condition. No aggregate, no committee, no state, ever constructed a castle in the clouds.

Mr. Foley, a partner in Schwabe, Williamson, and Wyatt, practices law in Portland, Oregon. He is a Trustee of The Foundation for Economic Education.

1. *Ron Paul's Freedom Report,* "The Elusive Dream for Great Leaders" (Vol. VIII, September 1983), pages 2–3.

2. In Nockean terms, the adept term is "state," not "society." Albert Jay Nock, *Our Enemy, The State* (Harper & Row Publishers, Inc., 1935).

3. Albert H. Hobbs, *Man Is Moral Choice* (Arlington House, New Rochelle, New York, 1979).

Freedom Promotes Integrity and Morality

by Bettina Bien Greaves

Throughout his many years of editing *The Freeman*, one of Paul Poirot's underlying motifs was that freedom helps to bring out the good in people. On the other hand, government intervention, coercion, tends to bring out the bad. Was this mere ivory-tower idealism, born of decades of seclusion in the sylvan dales of suburban Irvington? No! Rather it is solid realism, born of an understanding of human nature and the market process.

Given human nature, none of us will ever be perfect. There is good and bad in everyone. Every saint has in his makeup some flaw or human weakness, a little bit of the devil. Just as no one is perfect, however, so is no one 100 per cent evil either. No criminal is completely depraved, lost beyond all hope of redemption. Remember the maxim, honor among thieves. But most of us, Dr. Poirot maintained, will be better, more moral, if we live in a free society than if we live under collectivism.

A Free Society

A free society rests on the right to own property. As Dr. Poirot wrote some 35 years ago: "A man without property rights—without the right to the product of his own labor—is not a free man."[1] Only when man may own property and use it as he chooses is he free. If he is forced at gunpoint to devote his property to certain purposes, he is not free and deserves neither praise nor blame for the consequences. To be free a person must own property and dispose of it as he chooses.

In an article in *The Freeman*, Dr. Poirot pinpointed the clue to responsible human behavior and individual morality: "The personal freedom of choice that is liberty depends upon self-control and possession or ownership in the form of private property. And consistent with this concept of human dignity and private property is the right of the individual to make his own mistakes, if he so chooses, and to abide by the consequences."[2] Thus, responsible human behavior and individual morality both stem from the fact that under freedom the individual has "the right . . . to make his own mistakes" and the obligation "to abide by the consequences." These two factors bring out the best in man and help to keep him on the straight and narrow.

A person learns by trial and error. Mistakes teach caution, self-control, responsibility. Having to face the consequences of mistakes fosters moral values—cooperation, honesty, generosity. Government coercion has an opposite effect.

Collectivism

In an oft-cited chapter of *The Road to Serfdom,* F. A. Hayek explains "why the worst get on top" under collectivism. But it is not only to the top that the "worst" are attracted. The "worst" elements of society come to the fore at every level.

Often the only idea that will unite the masses is a negative emotion—hatred or envy of a common enemy. To attract the support of many, however, the rallying cry must appear to aim at a "higher goal," so hatred and envy are twisted to serve a "higher goal"—defense against a foreign foe, the preservation of racial purity, or the national economic welfare. This "higher goal" then comes to justify the means, any means. And the "plan" adopted to attain that goal must prevail, no matter its cost in money, forgone benefits, and human suffering.

Under collectivism, there is no morality except that prescribed by the collective. There is no loyalty except to the state. Traditional moral values are turned topsy-turvy. Children turn on their parents, brother on brother. An action is "good" or "bad" depending on whether or not it contributes to the "plan" or to the collective's "higher goal." Any means is justifiable, any lie permissible, if it contributes to the "plan" or the "higher goal." Members of the collective may engage in violent and immoral actions not permitted to them as separate individuals.

According to traditional standards of justice and morality general types of action are prescribed, others are proscribed. Good and bad stem from certain principles. "To cheat or steal, to torture or betray a confidence, is held to be bad. . . . Though we may sometimes be forced to choose between different evils, they remain evils."[3] In a collectivist state, however, cheating and stealing, torture and betrayal of confidence are not only tolerated but actually prized, if they promote the collective's "plan" or "higher goal."

Modern Interventionism

The modern interventionist society also violates traditional standards of justice and morality, although not to the same extent as does the totalitarian state. "Cheating" and "stealing" for the sake of the poor, the handicapped, rent-controlled tenants, beneficiaries of low-cost government loans, municipal planners, producers of certain agricultural commodities, and the like, have been made legal. "[T]he power of government is invoked to plunder property, ... [which] is a denial of the right to own and control property." This "is precisely how thieves operate: non-owners deciding how an owner may or may not use his property."[4]

Owners, deprived of the use of their property, are no longer free men. Their incentive to work, to produce, to save, and to invest is reduced. They no longer have the same incentive to avoid mistakes or the same responsibility to face the consequences. In this way, the interventionist state weakens individual initiative and erodes the moral fiber of the people.

Most interventionist programs are enacted with the best of intentions. They aim to help those who are unable to help themselves, to provide a "safety net" for those who fall through the cracks. However, these programs have the opposite effect from that intended. They discourage initiative, effort, and responsibility. They encourage more people to ask for help to seek to qualify for "safety net" benefits. Special interest groups are organized to demand "their rights." Welfare mothers clamor for more. To subsidize idleness is to shelter those subsidized from the consequences of earlier mistakes. It destroys the incentive of the less capable and less industrious. It also discourages their independence, fosters selfishness and the belief that the world owes them a living. Personal morality and family responsibility are eroded. Individual effort, initiative, and ambition are weakened. Moreover, the generosity of those who would have been willing to help is discouraged.

Standards of morality are also eroded when government tries to help businesses. If government engages in enterprises, grants credit, undertakes construction projects, contracts for services, offers aid to disaster victims, political favoritism is bound to play a role. Opportunities for bribery abound. Many fall for the "deep pockets" theory that no one will notice if government expense accounts are padded or bogus receipts issued for work that hasn't been done. Everybody's money is nobody's money. No one really cares if the costs of a project mount. The department or division chief need only return to Congress with a carefully formulated explanation as to why more money is needed for the "public welfare." Corruption runs rampant.

The Free Market

The daily newspapers are full of tales of crime, corruption, violence, and fraud. But most people are kind, generous, responsible, energetic, industrious, and productive. We learn very early in life that if we do something forbidden, we will be punished, but if we treat others well we will usually be rewarded. If we are kind, honest, and fair to family members, neighbors, associates, and even strangers with whom we have market dealings, they will usually show us similar respect in return. We can see widespread evidence of personal morality, integrity, and responsibility all around us.

People often give assistance to those in need of help. They contribute generously of their time and money to many worthy causes—the homeless, needy, lame, halt, blind, hungry, and poverty-stricken. Insofar as actions and transactions are voluntary, society reflects the humane side of human nature and fosters friendly interpersonal relations. Honesty, fairness, cooperation, generosity are usually reciprocated, upgrading the general morality of the community.

Freedom in economic affairs takes the form of a free market. Like freedom in general, the free market allows participants the freedom to choose and, thus, the freedom to make mistakes. But the free market also imposes on market participants the obligation to face the consequences of their mistakes. Thus, like freedom in general, freedom in economic affairs encourages responsibility and morality. Personal integrity, reliability, and responsibility are reflected in countless market transactions every day.

Successful Entrepreneurs Are Responsible Entrepreneurs

The entrepreneur who succeeds on the free market must have first of all an idea. He must supply consumers with some good or service they want. More than that, if he is to stay in business, consumers must value his product enough to pay a price that will cover all his costs—production, research, transport, and merchandising. The product must compete successfully with other products on the market in price, quality, and/or service. Some entrepreneurs appeal to consumers on price, others on quality, still others on service, still others on all three. But to succeed over the long run, customers must be convinced that an entrepreneur's good or service is as he represents it. Let's look at a few entrepreneurs whose businesses started small and grew by demonstrating integrity and reliability.

J. C. Penney

When J. C. Penney started his chain of stores he called them "Golden Rule Stores," and he tried to operate on that principle. His store managers became partners. "We were inspired," Penney later wrote, "by the consciousness that we were a fellowship every member of which was dependent upon the energy, integrity, and loyalty of every other member for security and success. . . . We operated in small towns and villages, and as small-town men we understood our new neighbors as readily as they understood us. It wasn't as if we had been a bunch of raiders swooping down upon them out of nowhere like the patent medicine and gold brick gentlemen who used to flash through that pioneering country for a quick cleanup and then disappear into nowhere. . . . We were among them to stay. We built upon their satisfaction and good will. If when they got their purchases home they were not fully satisfied, they knew they could always bring them back and receive their money, or a fair exchange, with courtesy and as a matter of course."[5] From a one-third interest in one small dry-goods store in Wyoming, Penney developed a chain of 1,600 stores with annual sales of more than $4 billion.

Henry Ford

By 1900, "horseless carriages" had been around for about fifty years but these early automobiles were expensive "toys" for the idle rich. Henry Ford worked as a young man for two automobile manufacturing companies that failed. Then he came up with the idea, considered crazy at the time, of producing an inexpensive car for the masses. He started his own business in 1903. His income soon exceeded his outgo. He plowed most of his earnings back into the business and expanded. Ford did not pretend that his car was as luxurious as the expensive autos of that day, but he offered reliability and integrity for the price. When his car was selling for $825, he boasted that "No car over $2,000 offers more except in trimmings," and many believed and bought. He persisted in his dream of producing an inexpensive car. In 1915, his Model T's sold for $440, and when his sales topped 300,000 he gave buyers a $50 refund. The price of a Ford continued to drop—to $290 in 1925—and its sales to increase. Ford's market share declined when competitors offered low-priced cars but his Model T had gained a solid reputation for reliability. However, when Ford's competitors began offering cars in various colors, and Ford stuck with black, he lost sales. But he learned from that mistake. The company researched other paints, retained its integrity and survived to earn profits again. The Edsel car, introduced in 1958, proved unpopular with car buyers, but the Ford Motor Company again bore the consequences of this mistake and recovered its reputation for producing reliable and desirable cars.

Sears, Roebuck and Co.

In 1886, Richard Sears was a railroad freight agent in North Redwood, Minnesota. A nearby jeweler refused a shipment of "yellow [gold-filled] watches," which sold in local stores for $25.00 each. The shipper let Sears purchase them at $12.00 each. Sears discovered he had a knack for writing advertising copy and sold them easily. He bought more watches and sold them, too. People began to ask him to repair watches. He advertised for a watch repairman and Alvah C. Roebuck answered the ad. The two joined forces and expanded the watch business. Sears "was no more honest than the other 'snake oil' salesmen of his time. But he was a lot better at writing advertising copy."[6] However, market competition helped to tame even Sears and to teach him integrity. He guaranteed his customers satisfaction, a replacement, or money refunded.[7] And "he always paid his bills promptly."[8]

In 1893, Sears and Roebuck established the mail order firm that bears their name. Roebuck couldn't stand Sears' high pressure selling tactics and pulled out. Sears found other more conservative business partners and the company kept expanding. Sears understood that "if you gouged the customer one year, you would lose him the next. So, . . . Sears, Roebuck bargained for lower prices from suppliers in return for making volume purchases. Then the company passed on the savings to the farmer." Sears' policy of low prices and satisfaction guaranteed or your money back earned the firm a loyal market.

Freedom Breeds Integrity

Countless firms have succeeded in our relatively free market by acting responsibly and morally. Countless voluntary agreements are made everyday that depend on the reliability and integrity of the parties concerned. Complex arrangements for the divison of labor and specialization are carried out, vast fortunes are traded, stock market purchases are made, contracts are fulfilled, huge buildings and skyscrapers are constructed, extensive fields are cultivated, long power lines and oil pipelines are laid, scientific research is conducted, goods are manufactured from resources and parts from many lands, countless commodities are sold to consumers in retail shops, credit transactions are fulfilled according to agreement, and so on. Most such voluntary transactions are completed honestly and fairly without serious controversy or friction. Most sellers offer satisfaction or your money back. A producer's label or trademark indicates his responsibility and willingness to stand behind the product.

Consumers are severe taskmasters. They want quality products at the lowest possible prices. They might be tricked into buying shoddy merchandise once but entrepreneurs who try that tactic soon realize that "honesty is the best policy." The tradesman or producer who tries to cheat or deceive his customers will not be in business very long. The only path to long-term profits on the free market is by serving consumers well, honestly, and fairly.

A Harmony of Interests

Under freedom people are united, not by a negative emotion, as under collectivism, but by a harmony of interests. They discover that they can accomplish many things through cooperation they couldn't do alone. People realize they can help themselves by being honest and fair with others. By conforming with the standards of justice and morality developed throughout the ages, everyone benefits.

Paul Poirot was correct when he wrote that freedom depends on self-control and private property, and that most of us have the potential for being better, more moral persons if we are free to own and to use our property as we choose, than if our use of property is restricted. The natural desire of people to be liked and to be successful creates pressures that bring out the salutary side of human nature. Freedom encourages individuals to treat one another with mutual respect and dignity, an attitude seldom encountered in the collectivist state. Out of the cooperation that develops among free men, an attitude of camaraderie emerges. Individuals recognize one another as unique human beings, with different ideas, talents, and interests, each of whom can make a contribution to society.

---

1. "Property Rights and Human Rights," *In Brief*, Foundation for Economic Education, 1952, p. 7. (Reprinted in *Essays on Liberty*, II, 1954, pp. 79–89.)

2. "The War on Property," in *The Freeman*, October 1967, p. 579.

3. F. A. Hayek, *The Road to Serfdom*, 1946, p. 146.

4. Poirot, *op. cit.*, pp. 582.

5. J. C. Penney, *The Man With a Thousand Partners: an Autobiography*, 1931, as quoted in John Brooks, ed., *The Autobiography of American Business*, 1974, pp. 75–76.

6. Gordon L. Weil, *Sears, Roebuck, U.S.A.: the Great American Catalog Store and How it Grew*, 1977, p. 12.

7. *Ibid.*, pp. 9–11.

8. *Ibid.*, p. 8.

Bettina Bien Greaves is a member of the senior staff of The Foundation for Economic Education.

Teachers of Liberty

BY PERRY E. GRESHAM

H. L. MENCKEN had a law something like Murphy's Law. Mencken's Law was "For every complex question there is a simple easy-to-understand wrong answer." Liberty involves a very complex question. Consequently, there are many wrong answers. The most obvious wrong answer is precipitous political action. The political process deals with power, and power is derived from public opinion. Politicians merely exploit the opinions that people already hold. If the people value and want liberty, then the political approach is possible. The question becomes "How can we interest the public in freedom?" Another wrong answer is that people are persuaded by argument. Political opinion is not turned by logical argument.

A partial right answer is education, but education is more than courses, lectures, libraries, and classes. The education which really makes a difference is individual learning. After fifty years of university teaching, I am convinced that nobody ever taught anybody anything. The truly great teacher is the person who catches the interest of the student and inspires the search for discovery. When the student feels the thrill of the quest for knowledge and discerns the dim outline of a new vision for liberty, then the process of learning is truly realized.

In one of Plato's dialogues, a student asks Socrates, "Can virtue be taught?" After much exchange of opinion and some cross-questioning, Socrates answers, "No, virtue cannot be taught, but if the gods are gracious, the young may learn virtue." Liberty cannot be taught, but if God is gracious, the student, the citizen, and the public may learn something of the value, the meaning, and the delights of liberty.

The truly great teachers are those who inspire their students, their colleagues, and the public to discover, learn, understand, and practice liberty.

Books, learned journals, seminars, university courses, public lectures, and opinions of thoughtful leaders have their place in promoting the freedom philosophy. Teachers, however, deserve special recognition for the role they play in starting the process of self-improvement which comes about as one studies and learns something of the meaning of liberty. Teachers can truly make a difference.

From many teachers I know, I have selected three who represent the powerful influence of great teaching. None of the three is still living. They have, in George Eliot's words, "joined the choir invisible of those immortal dead who live again in lives made better by their presence." Each one was a frequent contributor to *The Freeman,* and all were friends of Paul Poirot.

The economic legacy of Ludwig von Mises stands like a tall tower calling the universities of the world to learning and truth; his profound philosophy, his amazing wide-ranging knowledge of economics and human affairs, and his great intellect make him a paragon among those who inspire and teach graduate students and who determine the intellectual destiny of our age.

Benjamin Rogge exemplifies the noble tradition of college classroom teaching along with lecturing to business people, civic clubs, executive seminars, and consultation in the field of economics. Rogge spoke to the young and to the active participants in world economics and world affairs.

Leonard Read was the genial genius who startled the world with his versatility, his charm, his managerial skill, his facile pen, and his ability to inspire everyone who met him, whether it was face to face or from reading his engaging essays on freedom. FEE is the lengthened shadow of Leonard Read, lengthened further by his two teacher friends.

Ludwig Edler von Mises (1881–1973)

The exigencies of that dreadful Second World War caused one of the great Continental scholars and philosophers to leave his secure post as Professor at the University of Vienna and at the Graduate Institute of International Studies in Geneva. He came to America in 1940. With him came a solid philosophy of human existence which will serve as a touchstone for oncoming generations. He, in conjunction with Friedrich Hayek and Joseph Schumpeter, formed the great triad of Austrian economics in America.

The Mises bibliography is very impressive. *The Theory of Money and Credit* was published in 1912. *Socialism* (1922), *Liberalismus* (1927), *NationalOekonomie* (1940)—all these were published in Europe before he came to America. They still have readers throughout the Continent.

The world brotherhood of scholarly people made the Mises journey to America much easier. Henry Hazlitt, the famed economist, author, and columnist for *Newsweek* and *The New York Times,* had read something of Mises. Hazlitt and his close friend Larry Fertig helped Mises establish himself in New York City. Mises eventually obtained a teaching position at New York University. There he finished out his career as a visiting professor of economics and a lecturer to the great scholars of our time.

In 1949, the most famous of the Mises books, *Human Action—A Treatise on Economics*, was published by the Yale University Press. FEE subsidized the printing, and—in the pages of *The Freeman*—Leonard Read and Paul Poirot kept Mises before the public. The book is more than economics; it is an engaging philosophy of life.

Devoted students have much to do with the effectiveness of a teacher. The students of Adam Smith helped to make him famous. The students of Ludwig von Mises have carried the message throughout the land. Israel Kirzner is not only one of his most devoted disciples, but one of his most perceptive critics. Kirzner put together a handsome volume, *Method, Process, and Austrian Economics,* which is the result of his initiative to honor Mises on the 100th anniversary of his birth, September 29, 1981. This book includes the papers delivered at the C. V. Starr Center for Applied Economics at New York University. Eighteen papers and formal comments from students, colleagues, and critics of Mises constitute an impressive and persuasive collection of ideas in behalf of freedom. Kirzner summed it up when he said, "If we are the fortunate witnesses to a modest Austrian revival, this must certainly be attributed to the powerful influence of Mises' immensely persuasive teaching and writing."

Murray Rothbard, a devoted student of Mises, has made a considerable name for himself as a representative of the Austrian School of Economics. Some of the great lecturers at FEE and at other forums of freedom are former students of Professor Mises. They include Hans Sennholz, who has brought renown to Grove City College, and Bettina Bien Greaves, who, with her late husband Percy L. Greaves, Jr., has carried on at FEE the important lessons she learned at the feet of Ludwig von Mises. A beautiful biographical note comes from Margit von Mises, who shared the Mises pilgrimage. *My Years With Ludwig von Mises* is her moving story of a rare intellectual marriage and companionship.

Ludwig von Mises was denied, throughout his lifetime, the recognition which he deserves. He was not as widely known as a great university professor as he might have been had he taught at Oxford, Cambridge, Harvard, Yale, Chicago or any such prestigious university. He was given no world prize, such as the coveted Nobel. He had no organization to lengthen his shadow. He operated in a world climate in which socialism had cast a magic spell over many of the intellectuals. Yet, in his quiet way, he rediscovered the individual in economic thought. He brought America out of the miasma of the fascination with Marxism and the interventionist philosophy of John Maynard Keynes.

Benjamin Arnold Rogge (1920–1980)

I was attending a conference of businessmen, educators, and clergy sponsored by the National Association of Manufacturers in Bermuda.

One of the speakers was Benjamin Rogge. I was completely enchanted by the clarity of his powerful mind, the delightful surprise of his ready wit, the persuasiveness of his flawless logic, and the easy and articulate quality of his presentation. I forgot all about the beautiful out-of-doors and began to think about the persistent problems of the world economy. The president of NAM wanted to hire Ben Rogge on the spot. He graciously declined. Almost his entire career was invested in teaching at Wabash College.

Later, I shared the platform with Dr. Rogge at FEE seminars and at various business association meetings. We were natural friends from the beginning. We played golf together. Our wives were both fond of dancing and we attended many dances together. We were fellow board members of The Foundation for Economic Education.

I discovered that Ben Rogge had been born on a farm near Trumbull, Nebraska. Many farm boys then did not go to college, but Ben's teachers saw the promise of his bright mind and encouraged him to attend Hastings College, a college of liberal arts and sciences which had the advantage of offering an opportunity to learn without a great deal of expense and travel. He was such a success at Hastings College that his teachers and colleagues encouraged him to continue graduate study at the University of Nebraska. At the University, a wise and perceptive teacher identified Ben Rogge as a young man of unusual promise. The renowned School of Economics at Northwestern University was an opportunity for the young scholar to become a first-class economist certified by the diploma, Ph.D.

After a little time at the University of Nebraska and at the University of Wisconsin, he settled down at Crawfordsville, Indiana, where he was the very soul of economics at Wabash College. Business leaders from all over the world came to hear his lectures. His students were enthralled and went on to make names for themselves in the great universities. He was political scientist, philosopher, economist, and, for a short while, dean of the faculty. He was urged to become president, but graciously refused. Ben Rogge was a teacher. He would have been successful at administration, but it would not have been his natural talent, and he was shrewd enough to avoid the fearsome responsibilities that devoured some of us who made the mistake of spending years as college presidents.

Dr. Rogge was an early member of the Mont Pelerin Society. It was at a meeting in Switzerland that he met Leonard Read, the Founding President of The Foundation for Economic Education. Read heard Rogge's opinions on the subject, "Financing Higher Education in the United States." He was so taken by the young teacher/scholar that they became warm friends. Read incorporated Rogge into his Foundation for Economic Education; in fact, Rogge was practically the official lecturer for that institution.

On important anniversary events, Read always tapped Rogge to do the honors. He did them well and with precision. When he spoke, Adam Smith came to life and his "Natural Liberty" became self-evident.

Ben Rogge enjoyed lecturing and teaching more than writing. His solid book, *Can Capitalism Survive?*, is a collection of his able and appealing lectures. He narrated the films for "The Adam Smith Bicentennial," and for "The Incredible Bread Machine." With John Van Sickle, his Wabash colleague, he wrote an economic textbook which was used in many American colleges.

Rogge, like Mises, based his economic theories on individual responsibility for human action. He wrote,

> each man must be free to do what is his duty as he defines it, so long as he does not use force against another. . . . Each man [is] ultimately reponsible for what happens to him. True, he is influenced by his heredity, his environment, his subconscious, and by pure chance. But I insist that precisely what makes man man is his ability to rise above these influences, to change and determine his own destiny. If this be true, then it follows that each of us is terribly and inevitably and forever responsible for everything he does. The answer to the question, "Who's to blame?" is always, "*Mea culpa.* I am."

He went on to underscore the vital connection between economic and noneconomic freedom. According to Rogge, the noneconomic elements in total freedom—freedom of speech, of religion, of the press, and of personal behavior—"are not likely to be long preserved in a society that has denied economic freedom to its individual members."

Rogge did not harangue people, nor talk down to them. He challenged them to discover, to weigh and to consider. He had the confidence of John Milton that "as long as truth is in the field, we need fear no error." His life was not long. At sixty a malignancy had done its deadly work, but his influence continues in every one of his students, in all the business people who heard him speak, and in those of us who were his companions in the adventure toward understanding liberty.

Leonard Edward Read (1898–1983)

Some philosophers and savants who write history argue that times of great need bring forth great leaders. The cause of liberty was in such a time when the Second World War ended. The long administration of Franklin Delano Roosevelt had introduced America to the interventionist ideas of John Maynard Keynes. F.D.R. surrounded himself with Keynesian leaders. Among them was a popular economist named Stuart Chase, who was beguiled by the vast learning and winning prose of Lord Keynes. Socialism was popular in the United Kingdom, and the ideas came across the Atlantic.

George Santayana, in his book, *Character & Opinion in the United States*, wrote of the American, "When he has given his neighbour a chance he thinks he has done enough for him; but he feels it is an absolute duty to

41

do that. It will take some hammering to drive a coddling socialism into America."

That hammering was apparently accomplished during the Depression and World War II. America was in a socialist mood. Planning was the vogue. Social scientists talked of technocracy, whereby a few great brains could manipulate all the rest of us. *Laissez faire* was a very dirty word used to discredit anyone who believed in the market. The time was ripe for leadership.

Leonard Read, the organizational genius and the charismatic leader of the Los Angeles Chamber of Commerce talked the problems over with a few people, such as W. C. Mullendore, and broke away from the Chamber to start his own Foundation for Economic Education. Read was a truly great teacher, but unlike Mises and Rogge, he was not the product of the universities. His education, though adequate, was not remarkable. His greatness lay in the fact that he knew how to sense issues, gain perspective on the times, and institute action. His talents were numerous and amazing.

Will Rogers said, "I never met a man I didn't like." It could be said of Leonard Read that he met no one who didn't like him. He was so versatile, attractive, genial, and persuasive that the greatest leaders of America were drawn to him. Everywhere he went he inspired people to improve themselves in the study of liberty. Sometimes it would be on an airplane, where he logged a million miles and more; sometimes it would be in a conference; more often in one of his FEE seminars, where he gave that unforgettable lecture, "The Miracle of the Market." Everyone who met him was somehow involved in liberty.

He was unusual in that he would not argue. He had definite standards. He felt that a human transaction of ideas should involve learning; either he could learn from his interlocutor, or the companion could learn from him. There was no occasion for argument.

He did not try to be profound and learned. He laid hold of a few simple truths and held to them with the determination and strength of a pioneer defending his very life. On the day that I met him in Detroit, he was making a few remarks to the chief executives of the automobile industry. B. E. Hutchinson, financial executive of the Chrysler Corporation, was hosting the party. Present at the meeting were K. T. Keller of Chrysler, C. E. Wilson of General Motors, and Ernest Breech of the Ford Motor Company. Read's opening remark was, "Here are the three great moguls of the automobile industry, and not one of you knows how to make an automobile!" He went on to explain that nobody can really make anything without the division of labor.

This smashing point was beautifully developed in his little essay, "I, Pencil." This document alone covered the entire world. One of my academic colleagues who teaches in South Africa told me that it was even translated into Swahili. Milton Friedman made much of it in his popular book, *Free To Choose.* While Adam Smith gave long discourses on the manufacture of pins to demonstrate the division of labor, Leonard Read took a lead pencil and described it in such a way that no one who read or heard his remarks could ever forget.

I have said that Read attracted people. Some of the world's great labor leaders met him, heard him, and were inspired. He was particularly effective in winning powerful business executives to the cause of freedom. Even though he did not belong to the Groves of Academe, he was a hero to the mighty among the world's economists.

Coming to lecture at his foundation were such celebrities as Milton Friedman, Ludwig von Mises, Friedrich Hayek, David McCord Wright, Leo Wolman, Henry Hazlitt, Lawrence Fertig, Israel Kirzner, Yale Brozen, and a dozen others.

His appeal to celebrities brought such diverse and remarkable people as Maxwell Anderson, William F. Buckley Jr., Max Eastman, Russell Kirk, David Rockefeller, Henry Wriston, and Ronald Reagan to his cause. These people knew somehow that Leonard Read had gained rare insight into liberty, and they all wished to join in the search for more understanding.

Read wrote more than two dozen books; some of them very remarkable and important, such as *The Free Market and Its Enemy, Anything That's Peaceful,* and *The Coming Aristocracy.* Through his books he managed to convey the same intimate personal appeal that characterized his presence. His great sense of humor shines through the print. His perceptive and selective mind appears in the quality of people from whom he drew quotations.

One would expect a man of this quality to be versatile. He played golf very well and loved it; he won prizes for curling; he was a talented dancer; he was even talented as a gourmet cook!

He was a great conservationist; he loved every creature on this little blue planet. He romped with his dogs, fed the birds, refused to hunt, and even trained a pet skunk!

The change in the mood of America was somewhat influenced by the work of one man who explained that a person need not write, argue, and contend for liberty; but each person could advance the cause by simple self-improvement. My friend, Leroy Garrett, a philosophy teacher who publishes a small paper, wrote, "He never tried to reform others, only himself. Continual self-improvement was his rule, and he never stopped learning. He lived an exuberant life, mainly because he lived in a world of ideas, ideas that enriched and improved his life." Continued self-improvement was Read's rule, and he never stopped learning.

Small wonder that when Leonard Read died, pen in hand and still learning, President Ronald Reagan wrote, "Nancy and I send our heartfelt condolences on Leonard Read's death. We share your sorrow at the loss of a man whose dedication to our cherished principles of liberty burned brightly throughout his life. Our nation and her people have been vastly enriched by his devotion to the cause of freedom, and generations to come will look to Leonard Read for inspiration."

Legion are the teachers who join in the quest for liberty. These three great teachers I have mentioned are symbols of all teachers everywhere who make this world a freer and better place. It is small wonder that Marcus Aurelius, great stoic philosopher and emperor of Rome, began his book, *Meditations*, with a tribute to his teachers. Those of us who love liberty join in a tribute to all teachers everywhere who know what it means to be free.

Dr. Perry E. Gresham is President Emeritus and Distinguished Professor, Bethany College, Bethany, West Virginia.

Spontaneous Order and the Case for the Free Market

BY ISRAEL M. KIRZNER

THE case for the free society, it has widely and correctly been understood, rests in large measure on its economic achievements. It is demonstrated, through reference to history and by economic reasoning, that the free market has enormous potential for stimulating economic growth and prosperity. The proponents of classical liberalism can therefore argue that their idea not only respects the dignity, humanity, and moral worth of the individuals who make up society—it also promotes their economic well-being. Were it the case—as the enemies of freedom have again and again erroneously claimed—that absence of central economic planning constitutes a sure recipe for economic chaos and failure, it would be much more difficult to argue persuasively for the classical liberal society.

Many thoughtful observers might conclude that such supposed economic failings add up to too high a price to pay for the moral virtues of freedom. So it is eminently understandable that classical liberals have seen economic science, with its demonstrations of the economic advantages of free markets, as an important element in the intellectual struggle on behalf of the free society. While economic science itself may be value-free and quite independent of its role in the case for freedom, the ideology of freedom is fully justified in deploying the teachings of economics in promoting its cause.

To a considerable extent, the relevant lessons from economics revolve around the concept of *spontaneous order*. Whereas the untutored view of society is likely to assume that absence of central control must inevitably generate hopeless discoordination and frustration—economics shows how the opposite of this view is in fact the truth. Economics shows how, from the independent decisions of many market participants, there emerges a systematic process of learning and coordination. The outcome of this process is the spontaneous order of the market economy. It is upon this spontaneous order that the unprecedented prosperity of market economies rests. In recent years, particularly under the influence of Hayek's writings, a good deal of emphasis has come to be placed in the literature of liberty on this specific doctrine, the doctrine of spontaneous order.

The purpose of the present essay is to draw cautionary attention to a tendency to treat *all* examples of spontaneous order uncritically as equally powerful intellectual ammunition in developing the classical liberal case. I shall argue that this tendency is based on a serious misunderstanding. While it is emphatically true that the economic rationale for the free society rests largely on the notion of spontaneous order, it is *not* the case, I shall maintain, that every example of spontaneous order represents a useful weapon in the arsenal of freedom. In particular, I shall claim, a number of recent demonstrations that benign social conventions and institutions may have evolved organically and spontaneously have been thought to represent useful lessons pointing unequivocally towards the appreciation of the virtues of freedom. My position will be that it would be hazardous for proponents of freedom to rest their case substantially on such demonstrations. The critical policy issues facing modern societies are likely to be such, I believe, as at best to render quite irrelevant the lessons of social science concerning the long-run spontaneous emergence of benign social conventions. Proponents of freedom, it seems, would be well-advised to distinguish sharply between the kinds of spontaneous order that are generated in markets (against a given institutional background) and those other kinds of spontaneous order that may operate benignly to modify the institutional framework itself.

A prefatory word of clarification is perhaps called for. Nothing in what follows should be read as in any way critical of theories of long-run spontaneous order themselves. Such theories are highly stimulating, and a number of them may well be thoroughly valid and important. They may go far to illuminate significant aspects of human history. Our purpose here is to point out that reference to such studies may weaken, rather than strengthen, the economic argument for liberty. The economic argument for liberty rests on the propensity of markets to coordinate decisions and activities. The extraordinary power of arguments rooted in market theory should not be compromised by well-meaning but unhelpful reference to other kinds of spontaneous order. To point all this out is in no way to denigrate the profound scientific and human value of the long-run spontaneous order studies.[1]

Spontaneous Order: The Long Run and the Short

It is first necessary to articulate more sharply the distinction we wish to draw between two levels of, or dimensions for, spontaneous order. Traditional spontaneous order theorists from Ferguson and Smith onwards, generally assumed a society of individuals acting independently *within a given institutional framework*. That framework provided them with a relatively fixed background against which to operate. Economics then teaches that, under such conditions, a learning and discovery process is likely to be set in motion such as spontaneously to coordinate the independent actions of the participants. Without central control, participating individuals are led to anticipate each other's decisions correctly, yielding an orderly situation in which mutually advantageous exchange opportunities tend to become discovered and exploited for mutual benefit. The prime example of this kind of spontaneous order is the ability of a market to generate a tendency towards the market-clearing price. Clearly, the demonstration that such a tendency towards spontaneous order exists is of great significance for a society contemplating the avoidance of central economic planning.

What has been emphasized, on the other hand, in an important recent strand of literature, is the plausibility of long-run social processes— proceeding by and large *without* a fixed given institutional background— generating the gradual emergence of beneficial social conventions and institutions. Here, too, the outcome of these spontaneous processes is a state of affairs in which individuals correctly and confidently anticipate the actions and responses of other members of society. (It is this confidence that individuals have concerning what others will do that constitutes the conventions and institutions that are the spontaneous outcomes of these social processes.) In this sense, therefore, these long-run processes are "orderly"—they generate coordinated outcomes. Standard examples of such spontaneously achieved social conventions are language, standards of weights and measures, and codes of behavior among members of social groups.

These two kinds of spontaneous coordination process are, despite their shared features, fundamentally different from one another. The emergence within society of a common language, a common set of standards for weight and measurement, and common codes of social behavior, differs sharply from the emergence of a market-clearing price for wheat or for unskilled labor in competitive markets. The former are the results of long-run processes, lasting centuries, during the course of which we can presume many long periods of discoordination. The latter are relatively rapid processes. The former generate institutions—social signposts which facilitate subsequent social intercourse, but which do not themselves fulfill the final goals of individuals; these long-run processes result in the fulfillment of intermediate objectives only. The shorter-run process of spontaneous coordination may apply to the actions taken directly to fulfill final consumption objectives. The former, longer-run processes generate coordinated actions and responses which do not constitute interpersonal exchange transactions. (That different market participants use common conventions concerning quality, units of measure, and even the use of a common medium of exchange may indeed *facilitate* exchanges, but are themselves merely ancillary to such exchanges.) The shorter-run processes are processes generating mutually gainful exchanges between participants.

We shall argue that, from the perspective of defenders of the free society, these important differences point to vitally significant normative implications separating long-run processes of spontaneous coordination from the short-run processes: The former do not, while the latter do, in general lend support to the case for a free society.

Spontaneous Order and Social Welfare

The term "spontaneous order" is almost invariably taken to connote an outcome that is socially benign. There is indeed a sense in which this is likely to be true, but this sense is a quite limited one. No doubt it is in general desirable that individuals be able to arrive at confidently accurate anticipations concerning the actions and reactions of others. This avoids much disappointment and frustration on all sides. So that it is indeed useful that the language my children learn at home overlaps with the language learned by other children in *their* homes. This permits social intercourse and facilitates education. But there is hardly—in the insight that such institutions emerge spontaneously—any implication that the emerging institutions are the *best conceivable* such institutions. There is no guarantee that the English language my children learn at their mother's knee will be a "better" language for purposes of social intercourse than, say, French—or Esperanto. The demonstration that widely accepted social conventions can emerge without central authoritarian imposition does not necessarily point to any *optimality* in the resulting conventions.

What is demonstrated, on the other hand, by short-run spontaneous coordination theory (i.e., by the theory of the free market economy) is that there does exist a spontaneous tendency toward social optimality under the relevant conditions. The price that comes to be expected by all is not merely *any* price, but the *market-clearing* price, i.e., the price that stimulates the exploitation of the greatest possible volume of exchange opportunities. What is spontaneously tended to be achieved in these processes is not merely the avoidance of unrealizable anticipations, but the stimulation of anticipations that take advantage of conceivable opportunities.

Spontaneous Order and the Case for the Free Society

As noted at the outset of this essay, spontaneous order theory offers valuable ammunition for the proponent of the free society. Careful consideration of long-run processes of spontaneous coordination strongly suggests, however, that *these* processes not be cited as prime examples of what freedom can achieve. Awareness of these processes may indeed afford salutary refutation of naive prejudices concerning the chaos believed inevitably to ensue from the absence of central control. But such awareness is quite inadequate for building a general case for absence of centralized control. These processes cast much light on human history; but they offer little guidance for policy makers or social theorists pondering the foreseeable future. This is so for several reasons.

First, as noted in the preceding section, long-run spontaneous theory does not, in general, argue that evolved institutions are the best that might have come about. Second, long-run spontaneous theory does not, in general—there *are* exceptions—argue that deliberate centralized planning *could* not have arrived at equally benign (or better) social institutions. Third, because these processes are long-run in character, the benign character of the outcome may fall far short of justifying the process as a whole. After all, during the course of a centuries-long spontaneous process, there may occur (*conceivably* as a result of the absence of central control) a vast multitude of situations filled with human suffering and misery. It could be that the positive features of the resulting institution simply fail (no matter from *whose* perspective) to be judged worth these sacrifices.

Short-run processes of spontaneous coordination are far less vulnerable to such reservations. First, as noted, market processes tend, in general, to eliminate sub-optimalities. The relevance of Pareto-optimality to market processes is a systematic one. Second, market process theory not only shows how market coordination can be achieved spontaneously; it shows (as in the socialist calculation literature and related work) how such coordination could hardly be simulated by deliberate, central design. Third, because of the relative rapidity of market processes it is much more plausible to conclude that the optimality achieved by their outcomes justifies any sub-optimalities suffered (as a result of absence of control) during the process. (It must be recognized, however, that some of the institutions generated during long-run processes may continue to provide useful social services for a far longer period of time than can the market-clearing price achieved in a short-run market process.)

To recognize the limited relevance of long-run spontaneous processes for the theory of a free society is not to confess skepticism concerning the worthwhileness of such a society. After all, the traditional economic case for liberty rests not on possible long-term improvements in social institutions, but on the demonstrated advantages of liberty within a given institutional framework. A free society is prosperous, not because it generates a benign evolution in its laws, but because its given rule of law promotes innovative production and exchange. The classical case for freedom does not require that long-run spontaneous processes lead necessarily to better and better arrays of social institutions. In fact, for many proponents of the free society, its advantages depend on the fulfillment of limited but very definite assigned governmental functions. These governmental functions may well be assigned through explicit design. If the advantages of freedom *require* a framework of limited government, then one's assessment of the advantages of a centuries-long Nozickian process of freedom *without* a government may well be distinctly unfavorable—even if that process can be expected eventually to generate such limited governmental institutions.

But if all this is granted, then it should be pointed out that emphasis by proponents of classical liberalism on long-run spontaneous processes not only constitutes a weak reed on which to support their case—but in addition may itself *weaken* that case. Classical liberalism assumes an array of given institutions. To conflate classical liberalism with ideologies that call for no such given institutional framework is to sow confusion and misunderstanding. Out of such confusion and misunderstanding may emerge, not sympathy and appreciation for the free market society, but profound and unjustified skepticism of it. Efforts to broaden public understanding of the economic virtues of classical liberalism should, it very much appears, be undertaken with well-nigh exclusive emphasis of market processes with a given institutional framework. Reference to the possible spontaneous emergence of social institutions, where appropriate, should be made with careful clarification of their limited relevance for the economic case for the free society.

Dr. Kirzner is Professor of Economics at New York University and is a Trustee of The Foundation for Economic Education.

---

1. Among the works dealing with the spontaneous emergence or evolution of social norms and institutions see especially: Edina Ullmann-Margalit, "Invisible-Hand Explanations," *Synthese* 39, No. 2, (October, 1978), pp. 263–291; A. Schotter, *The Economic Theory of Social Institutions*, (Cambridge: Cambridge University Press, 1981); R. Axelrod, *The Evolution of Cooperation*, (New York: Basic Books, 1984); R. Sugden, *The Economics of Rights, Co-operation and Welfare*, (Oxford: Basil Blackwell, 1986). A good deal of Hayek's more recent work, especially his *Law, Legislation and Liberty*, 3 volumes (Chicago: University of Chicago Press, 1973, 1976, 1979), is steeped in this evolutionary perspective (and is probably partly responsible for the tendency being cautioned against in this essay).

Jeremiah's Job

BY GARY NORTH

SOONER or later, those who are interested in the philosophy of liberty run across Albert J. Nock's essay, "Isaiah's Job." Taking as an example two Old Testament prophets, Isaiah and Elijah, Nock makes at least two important points. *First,* until society seems to be disintegrating around our ears, not many people are going to listen to a critic who comes in the name of principled action. The masses want to get all the benefits of principled action, but they also want to continue to follow their unprincipled ways. They want the fruits but not the roots of morality. Therefore, they refuse to listen to prophets. *Second,* Nock pointed out, the prophet Elijah was convinced that he was the last of the faithful, or what Nock calls the Remnant. Not so, God told the prophet; He had kept seven thousand others from the rot of the day.

Elijah had no idea that there were this many faithful people left. He had not seen any of them. He had heard no reports of them. Yet here was God, telling him that they were out there. Thus, Nock concludes, it does no good to count heads. The people whose heads are available for counting are not the ones you ought to be interested in. Whether or not people listen is irrelevant; the important thing is that the prophet makes the message clear and consistent. He is not to water down the truth for the sake of mass appeal.

Nock's essay helps those of us who are used to the idea that we should measure our success by the number of people we convince. We are "scalp hunters," when we ought to be prophets. The prophets were not supposed to give the message out in order to win lots of public support. On the contrary, they were supposed to give the message for the sake of truth. They were to witness to a generation which would not respond to the message. The truth was therefore its own justification. Those who were supposed to hear, namely, the Remnant, would get the message, one way or the other. They were the people who counted. Lesson: the people who count can't be counted. Not by prophets, anyway.

A Sad Message

The main trouble I have with Nock's essay is that he excluded another very important prophet. That prophet was Jeremiah. He lived about 125 years after Isaiah, and God gave him virtually the same message. He was told to go to the highest leaders in the land, to the average man in the street, and to everyone in between, and proclaim the message. He was to tell them that they were in violation of basic moral law in everything they did, and that if they did not turn away from their false beliefs and wicked practices, they would see their society totally devastated. In this respect, Jeremiah's task was not fundamentally different from Isaiah's.

Nevertheless, there were some differences. Jeremiah also wrote (or dictated) a book: Lamentations. He was not content to preach an unpleasant message to skeptical and hostile people. He wanted to record the results of their unwillingness to listen. His thoughts are preserved in the saddest book in the Bible, the Book of Lamentations. Though he knew in advance that the masses would reject his message, he also knew that there would be great suffering in Israel because of their stiffnecked response. Furthermore, the Remnant would pay the same price in the short run. They, too, would be carried off into captivity. They, too, would lose their possessions and die in a foreign land. They would not be protected from disaster just because they happened to be decent people who were not immersed in the practices of their day. He wrote these words in response to the coming of the predicted judgment: "Mine eye runneth down with rivers of water for the destruction of the daughter of my people" (Lam. 3:48). He knew that their punishment was well deserved, yet he was also a part of them. The destruction was so great that not a glimmer of hope appears in the whole book.

What are we to conclude? That everything is hopeless? That no one will listen, ever, to the truth? That every society will eventually be ripe for judgment, and that this collapse will allow no one to escape? Is it useless, historically speaking, to serve in the Remnant? Are we forever to be ground down in the millstones of history?

One key incident in Jeremiah's life give us the answer. It appears in the thirty-second chapter of Jeremiah, a much-neglected passage. The abylonians (Chaldeans) have besieged Jerusalem. There was little doubt in anyone's mind that the city would fall to the invaders. God told Jeremiah that in the midst of this crisis, his cousin would approach him and make him an offer. He would offer Jeremiah the right, as a relative, to buy a particular field which was in the cousin's side of the family. Sure enough, the cousin arrived with just this offer. The cousin was "playing it smart." He was selling off a field that was about to fall into the hands of the enemy, and in exchange he would be given silver, a highly liquid, easily concealed, transportable form of capital—an international currency. Not bad for him, since all he would be giving up would be a piece of ground that the enemy would probably take over anyway.

Long-Range Planning

What were God's instructions to Jeremiah? *Buy the field.* So Jeremiah took his silver, and witnesses, and balances (honest money), and they made the transaction. Then Jeremiah instructed Baruch, a scribe, to record the evidence. (It may be that Jeremiah was illiterate, as were most men of his day.) Baruch was told by Jeremiah to put the evidences of the sale into an earthen vessel for long-term storage. "For thus saith the Lord of hosts, the God of Israel: Houses and fields and vineyards shall be possessed again in this land" (32:15).

God explained His purposes at the end of the chapter. Yes, the city would fall. Yes, the people would go into captivity. Yes, their sins had brought this upon them. But this is not the end of the story. "Behold, I will gather them out of all countries, whither I have driven them in mine anger, and in my fury, and in great wrath; and I will bring them again unto this place, and I will cause them to dwell safely: And they shall be my people, and I will be their God" (32:37–38). It doesn't stop there, either: "Like as I have brought all this great evil upon this people, so will I bring upon them all the good that I have promised them. And fields shall be bought in this land, whereof ye say, It is desolate without man or beast; it is given into the hand of the Chaldeans" (32:42–43).

What was God's message to Jeremiah? *There is hope for the long run for those who are faithful to His message.* There will eventually come a day when truth will win out, when law will reign supreme, when men will buy and sell, when contracts will be honored. "Men shall buy fields for money, and subscribe evidences, and seal them, and take witnesses in the land of Benjamin, and in the places about Jerusalem, and in the cities of Judah, and in the cities of the mountains, and in the cities of the valley, and in the cities of the south: for I will cause their captivity to return, saith the Lord" (32:44). In other words, business will return because the law of God will be understood and honored.

God had told them that they would be in captivity for seventy years. It would be long enough to make certain that Jeremiah would not be coming back to claim his field. Yet there was hope nonetheless. The prophet is not to imagine that all good things will come in his own day. He is not to be a short-term optimist. He is not to conclude that his words will turn everything around, making him the hero of the hour. He is told to look at the long run, to preach in the short run, and to go about his normal business. Plan for the future. Buy and sell. Continue to speak out when times are opportune. Tell anyone who will listen of the coming judgment, but remind them also that all is not lost forever just because everything seems to be lost today.

The Job Is to Be Honest

The prophet's job is to be honest. He must face the laws of reality. If bad principles lead to bad actions, then bad consequences will surely follow. These laws of reality cannot be underestimated. In fact, it is the prophet's task to reaffirm their validity by his message. He pulls no punches. Things are not "fairly bad" if morality is ignored or laughed at. Things are terrible, and people should understand this. Still, there is hope. Men can change their minds. The prophet knows that in "good" times, rebellious people usually don't change their minds. In fact, that most reluctant of prophets, Jonah, was so startled when the city of Nineveh repented that he pouted that the promised judgment never came, making him look like an idiot—an attitude which God reproached. But in the days of Elijah, Isaiah, and Jeremiah, the pragmatists of Israel were not about to turn back to the moral laws which had provided their prosperity. It would take seven decades of captivity to bring them, or rather their children and grandchildren, back to the truth.

Invest long-term, God told Jeremiah. Invest as if all were not lost. Invest as if your message, eventually, will bear fruit. Invest in the face of despair, when everyone is running scared. Invest for the benefit of your children and grandchildren. Invest as if everything doesn't depend on the prophet, since prophets, being men, are not omniscient or omnipotent. Invest as if moral law will one day be respected. Keep plugging away, even if you yourself will never live to see the people return to their senses and return to their land. Don't minimize the extent of the destruction. Don't rejoice at the plight of your enemies. Don't despair at the fact that the Remnant is caught in the whirlpool of destruction. Shed tears if you must, but most important, keep records. Plan for the future. Never give an inch.

A prophet is no Pollyanna, no Dr. Pangloss. He faces reality. Reality is his calling in life. To tell people things are terrible when they think everything is fine, and to offer hope when they think everything is lost. To tell the truth, whatever the cost, and not to let short-term considerations blur one's vision. The Remnant is there. The Remnant will survive. Eventually, the Remnant will become the masses, since truth will win out. But until that day, for which all prophets should rejoice, despite the fact that few will see its dawning, the prophet must do his best to understand reality and present it in the most effective way he knows how. That is Jeremiah's job.

Gary North is President of the Institute for Christian Economics, Tyler, Texas. He formerly served as Director of Seminars at The Foundation for Economic Education.

Vocation

BY EDMUND A. OPITZ

AROUND the turn of the century a great scholar named Max Weber produced a noteworthy study of the Reformation, and its aftermath, entitled *The Protestant Ethic and the Spirit of Capitalism*. Among other topics, Weber explored the religious idea of a "calling," or "vocation." The German word is *Beruf*.

During the centuries which antedate the Reformation we associate with the names of Luther and Calvin, the imperatives of a religious vocation drew the man or woman who felt the call to withdraw from worldly concerns and the workaday world into something like monastic or ascetic life. The Reformation, Weber contended, produced a dramatic broadening of spiritual orientation and outlook. The Reformation idea was to bring religion into the marketplace and forum; it "gave everyday activities a religious significance," as Weber put it. This new attitude toward our mundane and secular existence means that the craftsman or laborer who earns his daily bread by turning out honestly constructed and useful products is just as obedient to the will of God as is the man or woman in holy orders. This is a novel attitude toward economic life; industry and trade are now seen in a new light. From now on, as Francis Bacon put it, we do our daily tasks ". . . for the glory of the Creator and the relief of man's estate."

All useful work and every worthy occupation or profession may be invested with religious significance, that is, transformed into a "calling," by the worker's attitude toward whatever he does. Describing this attitude, Weber writes, ". . . every legitimate calling is exactly the same worth in the sight of God." The sixteenth-century poet George Herbert captures the mood in his oft quoted couplet, "Who sweeps a room as for Thy Laws/ Makes that and th'action fine."

Weber and his thesis came to mind as I reflected on Paul Poirot's attitude of quiet dedication and his low-keyed manner as he coped with the chore of editing *The Freeman*. He worked a seven-day-a-week job for thirty years.

For three hundred and sixty consecutive months this 64-page journal went out to tens of thousands of readers all over the world. This adds up to about twenty-one thousand pages of reading matter, more than ten million words, packaged attractively as more than three thousand solid, informative essays and about eight hundred book reviews. To give the journal permanence, bound volumes of *The Freeman*, carefully indexed, appeared annually. This six-foot stack of bound volumes is a compact but comprehensive little reference library of the freedom philosophy.

Such is the visible product, the effect. The cause operates backstage, so to say. Working behind the scenes, month after month for a generation, Paul had to sift through mounds of manuscripts to weed out the few that were publishable, soothe rejected authors with gentle rejection slips, edit the manuscripts he accepted, work with artists and printers who gave the journal eye appeal, put the issue to bed—and then, take a deep breath and start all over again on what would be next month's issue! And he did this without fanfare but with quiet dedication, fidelity to purpose, and philosophical integrity—every month for thirty years! If this does not have all the earmarks of a religious "calling" or "vocation," I do not know what does. Webster's Unabridged bears me out, offering a definition of "religious" which reads, in part, "scrupulously faithful or exact . . . conscientious." Some may object to the term "religious" in this broad, non-specific sense. So permit me to offer some speculations on the issues involved.

The average person hears the word "religion" and the image that comes immediately to mind is some variety of organized religion's formal expression, such as the red brick church on Main Street, or the white steeple house on the New England common, or the gray stone Gothic structure in the suburb. Or, the word may bring to mind such exotic world religions as Buddhism, Islam, Hinduism, or Confucianism.

Organized religion in the United States is rooted mainly in the Bible, and comes packaged in three major branches: Catholicism, Judaism, and Protestantism. These are theistic religions, that is, they affirm the reality of a sacred order that transcends the natural and social orders: a reality better characterized by a Thou than by an It. Theistic religions are rooted in the conviction that God is, and that God is spirit.

This is one answer to the question about the nature of ultimate reality; there are others. About a generation ago one of the signers of the original 1933 Humanist Manifesto, penned a pamphlet entitled "The Fourth R." The author coyly refers to the three traditional faiths of America— Protestantism, Catholicism, and Judaism—as our three "R's." But now, he argues, there is a fourth "R," Humanism, a religion which dispenses with God. Which is something like playing *Hamlet* without the Prince of Denmark! But Humanism does have other earmarks of a religion; its own creed, its own literature and liturgy, its own clergy and meeting places. The

American Humanist Association is the denominational structure of this fourth "R," and its very existence broadens the term "religion" far beyond what the seventeenth-century Puritan understood by religion.

Humanism is avowedly secular, but it is somewhat churchy and it does operate within the cultured and humane norms we associate with Western civilization. But no one would call secular Humanism a dynamic faith. There is, however, a dynamic faith on the move in today's world. The most widespread, fervent, fanatic, proselytizing, persecuting religion of the twentieth century is Communism. This is an evil religion for which men and women have died, and for which they are prepared to kill. Communism inspires in its votaries a dedication which other faiths might envy, but it is a destructive dedication to something less than the Most High—first-class dedication to a third-rate goal.

If Communism is a religion it is obvious that religion is not a thing limited to clergymen and church members. Virtually everyone has a "religion," not only those with ecclesiastical connections. This is not to say that everyone has what most people think of as religion. It is obvious that they don't, and the statistics bear this out. Nor am I saying that it is desirable that everyone have a religion; in the case of Communism and other fanatic creeds religion is undesirable, and even deadly.

Cosmic Concerns

In virtue of our very humanness, every man and woman is confronted with cosmic concerns, unique to our species, and demanding a response. There at least five such concerns, which may be best understood as questions. 1) What is the nature of this strange universe in which we find ourselves? What are its basic constituents? 2) What are the defining characteristics of the human species? What is our nature, really, and what is our destiny? 3) How shall we assess the fact of consciousness, mind, and reason in a largely material universe which is mostly devoid of anything like the mental? 4) What is right and what is wrong? 5) Does human life have a discernible meaning and purpose?

The people who wrestle with these questions are typically called philosophers and theologians, but the man in the street may work them over too. There are schools of thought grouped around the differing answers that have been given to questions like these, and virtually everyone has adopted one set of answers or another. Religion, then, may be defined as the basic response the human species works out to these five questions and their corollaries. Virtually every human being lives his life on the basis of his response to these urgent concerns, and thus almost no one is without a religion. But if it is not an intelligent response the results may be devastating.

Responses to these five concerns vary over a considerable spectrum, but here we can touch only briefly on the polar opposites, bearing the neutral labels theistic and non-theistic respectively.

1) What is the nature of the universe? The theistic answer runs somewhat as follows: There is in this universe a conscious, primal, creative thrust operating with intelligence, power, and purpose. This is the Divine Creativity, usually called God. In the material universe God is revealed in the orderly cause and effect realm of physical nature, where the laws of physics and chemistry reign. God discloses more of his workings in the biological realm of plants and animals; in the vitality, exuberance and adaptability of things that live. The most telling revelation of all is the human person, a work of divine art created in God's image, that is, gifted with the faculty of creative choice and the capacity for knowing his true nature and proper end.

2) and 3) What sort of a creature is man, and what is the status of mind, reason and free will? The theist maintains that man embodies a portion of the divine creativity, and thereby possesses free will. The primordial, purposive intelligence evolves man's brain and nervous system as a vehicle for his mind. His gift of reason is an ordered response to a rationally structured universe. The non-theistic alternative bows the knee to "omnipotent matter." In the oft quoted words of a famous philosopher, "Blind to good and evil, omnipotent matter rolls on its relentless way."

It follows, according to the non-theistic premise, that man is the accidental byproduct of physical and chemical reactions, as inexorably locked into nature's causal sequences as any other chemical compound. Human reason, then, is nothing but an irrational fact, the chance end result of the interaction of natural forces; and free will is an illusion. If man's will is not free, it follows that there is no human action; man can only *react*.

If something analogous to that in ourselves which we know as our own mind is not a fundamental fact of the universe, if mind is reduced to something engendered, willy-nilly, we know not how or why, from "omnipotent matter," then we have stripped mind of its credentials, discrediting any conclusions we might hope to reach by taking thought. Philosophers who strive to demonstrate that the mind is competent only to prove itself incompetent are a curious object for contemplation.

4) Right and wrong. The universe has an ethical dimension; it is so constructed, says the theist, that there is a right way for humans to live, and a wrong way. The moral distinction is not arbitrary, it cannot be altered, and it may be discovered by rational inquiry. The ages-old human quest for righteousness has left verbal deposits, such as the Ten Commandments, The Sermon on the Mount, the Golden Rule, and similar documents.

The non-theist envisions a universe of material particles, in the final analysis. Such a universe has no moral dimension. In the Marxist version of materialism the will of the party is supreme, and it is the party which decides what is right and wrong.

In the milder, Western version of materialism the pursuit of "enlightened self-interest" as a moral principle has had many advocates. If a person is advised to pursue his own interest he cannot be denied the right to decide for himself wherein his self-interest consists. For if A is allowed to define B's self-interest for him then B will be acting out A's interest and not his own. And of course no one would admit that his own interpretation of his self-interest is *un*enlightened! So everyone does "his own thing."

If the pursuit of self-interest is to seek one's good while staying within the rules, one has no quarrel with it. But the inordinate stress on self-interest gained its ascendancy precisely because of the decline of belief in a universe with a moral dimension; what some call the Natural Law. And that gets us into trouble. If every individual pursues his own interest, or seeks his private advantage, or does his own thing, it is impossible from this starting point to arrive at any sort of a general rule, or principle, or ethical norm. X might *call* something a principle or norm, but only because his self-interest dictates that he do so; or doing so gains him some private advantage. And if there are no rules, why should A, having been told to pursue self-interest, refrain from initiating force when his rational calculation of costs and benefits determines that the benefits of aggression far outweigh any costs that may accrue. Tomorrow, the situation may have changed and, in this new situation his self-interest may dictate that he inveigh heavily against the initiation of force! When the crunch comes there is no substitute for the time-tested moral code whose mandates form the necessary foundation of a free society: Don't murder; Don't steal; Don't assault; Keep your word; Fulfill your contracts.

5) "Into this universe, and why not knowing / Nor whence, like water willy-nilly flowing." So sang old Omar, echoing the ancient non-theistic conclusion that man is a chance excrescence thrown up on the surface of the earth by forces he cannot even comprehend, let alone control to further his own purposes. According to the non-theistic or materialist philosophy there is nothing in the universe that shares man's values or responds to his aspirations. Man is a waif in an alien universe, buffeted by forces he cannot comprehend, doomed at last to complete his pointless journey with as little distinction as he began it, his proudest achievements reduced to dust and forgotten. The mood of our time is begotten by this world view, and the mood is a compound of sadness, resignation, rebellion, defiance, and despair.

There is no reason to assume that our species will ever know more than a fraction of what there is to be known: "We see as through a glass, darkly," wrote the early Paul nearly two thousand years ago. Questions about the meaning and purpose of human life are not to be resolved after the manner of a Euclidean demonstration, nor is there any conceivable scientific experiment that might tell us whether or not life is worth living. The theistic world view, in short, has no prepackaged answers, but it does tell us that the human species is meaningfully linked to the Creative Intelligence which transcends all things. Choose to live so as to strengthen that link and a kind of divine alchemy causes the universe to respond and confirm the wisdom of our decision.

The Reverend Mr. Opitz is a member of the senior staff of The Foundation for Economic Education, a seminar lecturer, and author of the book, Religion and Capitalism: Allies, Not Enemies.

This I Believe . . .

BY WILLIAM H. PETERSON

I BELIEVE that economic freedom and political freedom are indivisible, that neither can exist without the other, that economic democracy and political democracy are both governed by individual choice—the one in the marketplace and the other in the polling booth—that if capitalism did not exist it would be necessary to invent it.

I believe that human rights rest on private property rights, that your home is your castle, that your greatest property or trust is yourself, that civil rights and property rights are inseparably joined, that liberty and privacy are two sides of the same coin.

I believe that rights confer duties, that liberty without conscience, without moral obligation, becomes license, that freedom requires civility and decorum and sensitivity for the rights of others, that it calls for, ideally, cheerfulness, that life is after all a celebration. I believe that duty is personal, that we are individually, privately, our brother's keeper, that the three ultimate Rs are reverence, respect, and responsibility.

I believe in the individual, in his dignity, uniqueness, and potential. Organization is necessary but I place the individual above the organization, and hold that only the individual can feel and think and truly choose and act. I believe that an organization—including society and the family—is in essence an aggregation of individuals, each with a mind of his own, that any organization is the product of individuals, of human design, of human action, that the direction of that organization is in the hands of those individuals—in their leadership, their minds, their ideas, their philosophies, their esprit de corps, their sense of obligation to each other.

I believe in the power of choice, of the human mind, for good or evil, that the mind, perceiving cause and effect, rightly or wrongly, directs choices—including, in the words of Ludwig von Mises, "the sublime and the base, the noble and the ignoble." I believe that the mind can be moved by ideas, the young mind more so, and hence that the role of education, of the transmission of accumulated knowledge and wisdom, is critical to the course of human events.

I believe that your future is what you make it, that as you invest in yourself so your potential rises, that you can will your will, that man is the architect of his lot and not the prisoner of his environment—that character is destiny. I believe with Einstein that God does not play dice with the world, that chance plays but a secondary role in life and history.

I believe that history, whether personal or organizational or national, is not the result of blind forces but the product of the human mind, of human action. I believe that it is good and bad ideas, values, customs, institutions, and traditions—including the tyranny of the status quo, to borrow the phrase of Rose and Milton Friedman—that shape the present and the future rather than the other way around.

I believe in the creative individual, in what Shakespeare said of man some four centuries ago: "How noble in reason! how infinite in faculty! in form and moving how express and admirable! in action how like an angel! in apprehension how like a god!" Or in what Alexis de Tocqueville said in *Democracy in America* some 150 years ago: "No natural boundary seems to be set to the efforts of man, and in his eyes what is not yet done is only what he has not yet attempted to do."

I believe in entrepreneurship. The entrepreneur is the spark, the leader, the innovator who creates new resources, new products, new services, new production techniques, new marketing methods, new financial tools, new industries, new jobs—all those new and better ways to serve mankind. The entrepreneur, under competition, is the agent and, in effect, the employee of the sovereign consumer who, through the power of the purse, rules the marketplace.

I believe in free trade, in voluntary and mutually beneficial exchanges, whether domestic or international. I believe that merchants are ambassadors of good will, of economic development, that the road to world peace lies in world trade, that, in the dictum of French economist Frederic Bastiat, "when goods can't cross frontiers, armies will."

I believe in Adam Smith's concept of "the invisible hand" as the quintessence of free enterprise, that as you pursue your self-interest in the marketplace, in the absence of fraud or force, you necessarily cooperate with others—indeed, consciously or unconsciously cater to their wants—and thus help achieve a spontaneous economic order and serve the public interest, the common good, the greatest happiness for the greatest number.

I believe in Jean Baptiste Say's "law of markets" as also the quintessence of free enterprise, that supply creates equivalent demand, that in the marketplace, and in the human mind, trade-offs prevail, always, that to get you must give, that something is only for something, nothing is ever for nothing—that there is no free lunch, never.

This I Believe . . .

I believe in government, but in constitutionally limited government, in government whose guiding principle for civil behavior is, as Leonard Read put it, anything that's peaceful, in government by law as opposed to government by men, in the idea that government intervention in peaceful private activity tends to make things worse rather than better. I believe that government alone possesses the double-edged sword of the legal power of coercion, that lawmakers, majorities, and minorities, like individuals, can advance social cooperation—i.e., peace and prosperity—or they can fall prey to fallacy, to what F. A. Hayek calls "the pretense of knowledge," to policies leading to failure or disaster, to the corruptibility of power, especially the power to tax, to build bureaucratic empires, buy votes, and subvert the independent citizen.

There are more beliefs, of course. But these, to me, are at the heart of the American Constitutional system of free markets, private property, and government constrained by checks and balances, as envisioned and bequeathed by the Constitutional Framers 200 years ago.

Professor Peterson is a senior fellow at the Heritage Foundation in Washington, D.C.

Law, Economics, and Freedom

BY SYLVESTER PETRO

THE IDEA OF freedom has for millennia fascinated thinkers ranging from monarchs to metaphysicians. Natural scientists, ethicists, moralists, jurists, philosophers, general intellectuals—have tried their hands. Economists, especially, tend to write and speak as though the subject belongs peculiarly to them, possibly because they think of the free market as an economic institution.

However, lawyers, judges, and legal institutions carry the responsibility, for better or (too often) for worse, of administering freedom in society. It falls to them to set the metes and bounds of freedom, just as it falls to them to settle all other boundary disputes, all the conflicts dealt with by property, contract, and tort law.

Scientists, philosophers, and economists have had to put in cold storage their analysis and development of the ideas of freedom when the going gets rough and practical action is required. No matter how much their disciplines might contribute to the amplification of the idea of freedom, they, *as such*, have had no jurisdiction, no authority, no practical role in the administration of freedom in crises. When human beings can take no more, when they finally find control of their persons or their possessions—their freedom—intolerably invaded, they resort to arms, not to philosophers, not even to economists. They wield sticks and stones, guns, swords, tooth and claw, when there is nothing else, as the Hungarians did in 1956. But they will prefer to resort to the arms hidden in legal institutions, if those institutions are available and in decent working order.

It is not surprising, therefore, that such definite contours as personal freedom possesses are traceable today to decisions that have been handed down by courts. Philosophers and others have perhaps evolved the best general definition of freedom—in John Stuart Mill's words: "The only freedom which deserves the name, is that of pursuing our own good in our own way, so long as we do not attempt to deprive others of theirs, or impede their efforts to obtain it." But I doubt that they would ever have arrived at even that definition had it not been for the long years of juridical experience that preceded it. Moreover, the guidance provided by this definition is limited; it leaves the law with challenging problems in deciding in concrete cases when the pursuit of "our own good" deprives others of theirs; when, in fact, our actions invade rather than exercise freedom. If without reasonable justification your neighbor disturbs your slumbers, is he exercising *his* or invading *your* freedom?

The "Paradoxes of Freedom"

These deceptively simple issues, daily fare in the law, are hellishly difficult to resolve. But I propose to do the best I can to indicate how the law goes about resolving what statists like to call the "paradoxes of freedom."

Abstract "natural rights" thinking helps so little at this point that jurists have often thrown up their hands in despair, as Jeremy Bentham did, calling the whole mode of thought useless as even a mere starting point in the practical administration of justice.

Closer to home, Ludwig von Mises (whose degree was in law) turned his brilliant lamp briefly on the question, seeking freedom's first principle, and illuminated one of its deepest shadows by pointing out that the issue of freedom could never arise except in ordered society, and that, therefore, there is no point in talking about it in the state of nature. He said:

> Freedom and liberty are not to be found in nature. In nature there is no phenomenon to which these terms could be meaningfully applied. Whatever man does, he can never free himself from the restraints which nature imposes upon him. If he wants to succeed in acting, he must submit unconditionally to the laws of nature.
>
> Freedom and liberty always refer to interhuman relations. A man is free as far as he can live and get on without being at the mercy of arbitrary decisions on the part of other people. In the frame of society everybody depends upon his fellow citizens. Social man cannot become independent without forsaking all the advantages of social cooperation. The self-sufficient individual is independent, but he is not free. He is at the mercy of everybody who is stronger than himself. The stronger fellow has the power to kill him with impunity. It is therefore nonsense to rant about an alleged "natural" and "inborn" freedom which people are supposed to have enjoyed in the ages preceding the emergence of social bonds. Man was not created free; what freedom he may possess has been given to him by society. Only societal conditions can present a man with an orbit within the limits of which he can obtain liberty. (*Human Action*, pp. 279–80)

Mises goes on to say that "Freedom as people enjoyed it in the democratic countries of Western civilization in the years of the old liberalism's triumph, was not a product of constitutions, bills of rights, laws, and statutes. Those documents aimed only at safeguarding liberty and freedom, firmly established by the operation of the market economy, against encroachments on the part of officeholders. No government and no civil law can guarantee and bring about freedom otherwise than by supporting and defending the fundamental institutions of the market economy . . . Where there is no market economy, the best-intentioned provisions of constitutions and laws remain a dead letter." (*Ibid.*, p. 283)

In opposing government to freedom in this statement, Mises has apparently slipped a cog. For what if the "fundamental institutions of the market economy" are themselves products of law and government? If private property and freedom of contract, the institutions that Mises himself (p. 280) calls the framework of the market economy, are juristic principles— creatures of kings, of the judges they appointed, and of the legislatures— why not recognize the state as the friend of freedom rather than treat it as an implacable enemy?

Another legally trained European, Bruno Leoni (but he more lawyer than economist), pointed out the problem in this part of Mises' analysis. He emphasized that the market economy is nothing if not a legal institution. In *Freedom and the Law* he said:

> The free market . . . inevitably implies the idea of a "constraint" in that all the members of a market society have the power to exercise restraint against people like robbers or thieves. There is no such thing as a free market with some constraining power superadded. A free market is rooted in a situation in which those engaged in market transactions have some power to constrain the enemies of a free market. This point probably is not emphasized sufficiently by those authors who, in focusing their attention on the free market, end by treating it as the very antithesis of government restraint.
>
> Thus, for instance, Professor Mises . . . says that "liberty and freedom are terms employed for the description of the social conditions of the individual members of a market society in which the power of the indispensable hegemonic bond, the state, is curbed lest the operation of the market be endangered." We notice here that he has qualified as "indispensable" the hegemonic bond of the state, but he means by liberty, as he also says, "restraint imposed upon the exercise of the police power" without adding exactly, as I would consider it reasonable to add from the point of view of a free trader, that liberty means also restraint imposed on the exercise of the power of anyone else to interfere with the free market. As soon as we admit this meaning of liberty, the hegemonic bond of the state is not only something to be curbed, but also, and I would say *first of all*, something we make use of to curb other people's actions. (*Freedom and the Law*, pp. 49–50)

I accused Mises a moment ago only of slipping a cog because he fully understood the role that private property and freedom of contract play in the market economy. He himself said in *Human Action* that "[1] liberty and freedom are the conditions of man within a contractual society." (*Human Action*, p. 280). And there can be no doubt that Mises was aware of the juristic character of contract. There can be promises, perhaps, in the "state of nature." But a contract is an *enforceable* promise, and enforcement implies the state and legal institutions, as Mises very well knew.

Thus, while Mises may have slipped a cog, Leoni's criticism was not free of pettifoggery. It is true that in the passage quoted by Leoni, Mises seems to have regarded the state as exclusively the opponent of freedom, and in no sense its protagonist. But there can be no question in the mind of anyone who has read him fully and fairly that Mises had a perfect grasp of the positive relationship between law and freedom. He was fully aware that such private persons as union thugs, can invade freedom as savagely as the state can. He said: "The self-sufficient individual is independent, but he is not free. He is at the mercy of everybody who is stronger than himself. The stronger fellow has the power to kill him with impunity [in the state of nature]." Mises thought that the state—the "indispensable hegemonic bond"—is as indispensable to freedom as it is perilous; that the police can be both friend and foe of freedom, *as every other human being can be.* He may have loathed and distrusted the state, but he distrusted the state of nature—anarchy—even more.

Seeking the Ultimate Source of Our Liberties

To say that the law is the guarantor of our liberties, it must be emphasized, is not to say that it is also the *ultimate source.* That source is as inscrutable as the prime mover of the universe. We can verbalize the obscurity—trace it back into the human mind, the human spirit, the "soul," if you prefer. I have myself said that freedom, well-being, and security are the built-in, the ultimate, human values. (See *The Labor Policy of the Free Society* [1957].) But I believe that objective, nonmetaphysical analysis must stop with some such self-evident postulate. We are capable of such words and ideas as "God," "nature," "divine consciousness," but they seem to me to be invitations to argument rather than clarifications. Efforts by Nozick and Epstein to trace back property and contract and liberty to more primal sources seem to me to be bootless whistling in the dark.

In any event, I content myself here with the profound concept of the commonwealth stated by Dante Alighieri in *De Monarchia*— "The aim of rightful commonwealths is liberty, to wit that men may live for their own sake," and with the intimately related definition of law offered by Thomas Aquinas: "an ordinance of reason directed to the common good," with the common good being defined as freedom, well-being, and security, the ends that Western man has sought.

Reflection on this conception of law and the common good suggests that the "fumbling around" theory of legal development associated with Edmund Burke and Friedrich Hayek does not amount to much. Certainly, no one can deny that the legal institutions and principles of the Western world have had their ups and downs; or that it has taken centuries for them to fix on a direction and to follow it with some consistency. But no one in his right mind expects perfection from any human being or any institution—in any field of human action. Of course, the law has fumbled around. But fumbling, too, can be a rational activity; trial and error is not only a rational methodology, it is about the best and most rational one available to mankind, in all areas of human action, including "scientific" laboratories.

Bear in mind here the remarkable fact that all over the West the legal institutions came roughly to the same conclusions at roughly the same time. In all Western countries, the "common good" to which their *reason* directed them was *freedom and its handmaidens, property and contract,* good not only in themselves but also in the well-being and security they promoted by way of increasingly free markets. The actual historical process was endlessly complicated, tragic, full of false moves, crammed with good results from bad motives and bad results from well-motivated actions. And yet, from it all, there emerged the most useful and productive juridical principles ever conceived: private property and freedom of contract.

Sir Henry Maine was simply summing up these developments when he said that "the movement in the progressive societies has hitherto been a movement *from status to contract.*" In saying this, he was not only stating a fact; he was also challenging Burke's muddled anti-rationalism. The pursuit of freedom, well-being, and security—man's ultimate social values—was about as deliberate as it could very well be. And Maine's dictum was not confined to England, or France, or even to Europe. As he stated it, it applied to *all* progressive societies.

It fell to the best court of this country in 1870, about the same time that Maine was writing, to say in an important decision that:

> Freedom is the policy of this country. But freedom does not imply a right in one person, either alone or in combination with others, to disturb or annoy another, either directly or indirectly in his lawful business or occupation, or to threaten him with annoyance or injury, for the sake of compelling him to buy his peace; or . . . to compel him to do any act against his will. The acts alleged and proved in this case [extortionate strike-threats] are peculiarly offensive to the free principles which prevail in this country; and if such practices could enjoy impunity, they would tend to establish a tyranny of irresponsible persons over labor and mechanical business which would be extremely injurious to both."(*Carew* v *Rutherford*, 106 Mass. 1, 15)

Carew v *Rutherford*, like a thousand other decisions that might be cited, reveals how the common-law judges of this country, when their heads were clearer than they are now, were systematically, that is, rationally (not blindly), developing our free institutions. At the same time it serves to expose some deficiencies in current libertarian thought about freedom. I am thinking here of the libertarian belief that in order to be free persons must be privileged to engage in any activity so long as it is peaceful, the equally widespread libertarian notion that some types of action are or should be absolutely privileged, and the quasi-libertarian idea that the common law courts took as their guiding principle of decision that it was the function of law to maximize wealth.

Anything That's Peaceful?

Perhaps the most seriously defective of these libertarian beliefs was summed up in the title of one of Leonard Read's books, *Anything That's Peaceful*. The shortcomings of this formula are sharply brought out in the thousands of court decisions holding wrongful many kinds of peaceful acts ranging from deception, to blackmail, to passing off one's goods as those of another, to spite fences, to diversion of streams solely in order to hurt one's neighbor, to such extortionate strike-threats as were held wrongful in *Carew*, to peacefully inducing one party to break his contracts with another, and, in general to secondary boycotts.

This is not the place for an exhaustive coverage of all these examples of peaceful wrongdoing, so let us be content with the strike-threat in *Carew* as an illustration. Prima facie, peaceful strikes were held to be acts of privileged freedom at common law. Yet the judges were very often confronted with instances in which such strikes did the kind of harm that a legal system intent on advancing freedom could not tolerate. Therefore, for the reasons set forth in the quotation above from *Carew*, the court held the strike-threat wrongful.

This case by itself shows that no legal system intent upon maximizing freedom could possibly hold every kind of peaceful act, privileged. However, it has a lot more than that to teach.

The *Carew* case serves well also to expose the deficiency in the belief that freedom requires absolutely privileged status for certain activities. One would think that if any act should be absolutely privileged, certainly a simple refusal to work should be—for is not the essence of slavery and the antithesis of liberty the activity known as forced labor? In order to display the weakness in this view, and in the belief that some acts should be absolutely privileged, I quote here a small part of one of the most incisive pieces of legal analysis I have ever encountered. The writer was Professor William Draper Lewis, and the article was in the *Harvard Law Review* of 1905 (pp. 449–50):

> The act of selling one's labor or one's goods is an act which in the past has usually gone unquestioned, because it was never performed under circumstances which shocked the moral sense of the community. The idea that there is an inherent right to buy or sell, to work or not to work as one pleases, was the natural result. But the act of selling one's labor or one's goods does not differ essentially from any other act. There is no less and no more inherent right to sell labor or goods than to chop a tree. The legality of the act of tree-chopping depends on the surrounding circumstances; so with the sale. The law of torts in the past has not sprung, and could not spring, from an examination [only] of the rights of those who injured others.

Professor Lewis's powerful point, often overlooked in the legal literature, was that freedom is a two-sided affair, as the valuable dictum of John Stuart

Mill, quoted earlier, declares. Personal freedom extends only to the point where it infringes the freedom of others. At that point there can be no absolute privilege. There must be accommodation of equal rights and privileges and immunities. If taking a breath at a certain time and place is designed to hurt someone else, even that may be an invasion rather than an exercise of freedom, and so too with every other conceivable peaceful act. And any legal system which stopped in such circumstances with evaluating the right to breathe in the abstract, without inquiring into the purpose and effect of a deep breath which just happened to kill someone else, would be a stupid enemy of freedom, not its servant.

The fact that emerges from long legal experience is that *no* act can be regarded as absolutely privileged, regardless of time, place, circumstance, intention, and consequential harm to others. If *no* act can be absolutely privileged, it goes without saying that many kinds of peaceful conduct can constitute wrongful and actionable invasions of freedom.

This conclusion, by the way, provides an essential clue to the way in which systematic jurisprudence may be admitted into the ranks of the sciences of human action, praxeology, the discipline that encompasses all purposive conduct. As a great jurist, Professor N. Korkunov, pointed out in his *General Theory of Law* (N.Y.: Macmillan Company 1922, p. 42), law and its norms are all ends-oriented. They are not concerned essentially with the facts or even with the principles related to the arts and sciences. As Mises would have it for all praxeology, the law too is essentially teleological; it looks not only to the purpose and effect of actions but to the social ends that its rules and principles serve:

> Man cannot guide himself through life [said Korkunov] merely by technical norms [e.g., engineering principles] suited only to the attainment of separate ends. He is guided necessarily by another principle which determines the choice of ends themselves . . .
> . . . Technical norms are the rules directly applicable to the realization of the distinct ends of human activity, ethical norms [i.e., the rules of law] to the realization simultaneously of all human ends.

And this is why in filling its role as an ordinance of reason directed to the common good, the law must constantly be preoccupied with the teleological components of the facts which it confronts daily. It must look to the purpose of the actor and to the effects of his actions on the purposes of the other party, the victim, the person injured.

Law and Economics

In recent years the idea has been advanced by a number of lawyers who fancy themselves economists as well, that our legal system either has, or should have, maximizing wealth as its main objective—not maximizing freedom or any other version of the "common good."

This is a big subject. To do it justice would require much more time and space than is available to me now. Yet I cannot resist saying a few words about it.

I wish to say in the first place that the idea cannot pass muster as an accurate account of either what the common law judges thought they were doing or of what they actually did. In thousands of cases, especially "nuisance" cases, large mining and manufacturing firms tried to defend themselves in suits brought by homeowners, small farmers, and others suffering physical harm, by proving to the courts that the harm they did was infinitely smaller than the wealth they created. Once in a while a court would accept such a defense. But as a rule the judges rejected the notion that harm to one party's property rights could be justified by the other party's greater productivity. See, for example, *Arizona Copper Co.* v. *Gillespie*, 12 Ariz. 190, 203, 100 Pac. 465, 470 [1909].

I would suggest in the second place that it is bad economics to believe that social wealth can be increased by tolerating conduct that destroys the property and freedom of others, even if it results in greater wealth for the actor. Besides amounting to a justification of the acts of muggers, embezzlers, and burglars, it also misconceives the nature of wealth. Wealth is a subjective thing, as economists of all schools have come to realize. More than that, wealth is not confined to material possessions. A man who possesses few or no material goods can be as well off as a person who owns so many material goods that he cannot even count them. He might even be better off.

Consider the case of the owner of an acre of vacant land on 5th Avenue and 42nd Street in Manhattan who refuses to sell it for millions, even though the buyer would use it in an extremely productive enterprise, while the owner lets it lie vacant. Would the wealth of society be increased by forcing the owner to sell? I asked an economist of the positivist Chicago School that question once. He gave the right answer: "of course not." But I wonder whether he realized just how sharply his correct answer refuted the positivist economics associated with the Chicago School.

The trouble with the idea that judges should be driven by wealth-maximizing objectives runs very deeply. I wish to say in the third place that it misconceives the nature of law. Without understanding the nature of either law or economics, it would nevertheless hold that law is a branch of economics. But law can no more be identified with economics than it can with any other truth-seeking activity. Law does not seek truth except as a means to gain its larger ethical ends. Its aim is justice, not wealth, and it aims at justice because its ultimate function is to promote social peace and harmony.

So far, social peace and harmony have tended to promote the increase of creature comforts, and life has grown longer with more material goods. But these results, however good or bad they may seem, do not prove that the role of law is to increase physical wealth; only that when people have lived in a regime of peaceful freedom they have tended thus far to prefer goods-increasing activities to more leisure, to quietism, or to a mindless descent back into the primal slime. A legal system successfully producing peace and harmony in a society dominated by values contrary to those prevailing *thus far* in the West will produce other results, perhaps even the disintegration of human society.

It is as absurd to view the law as a branch of economics as it would be to view it as a branch of physics or chemistry merely because judges must often resort to the laws and the truths uncovered by those disciplines in order to decide certain cases properly. Law is a moral-ethical activity preoccupied with *what ought to be*—and with what *is* only incidentally to its main purpose. Like religion, which is also concerned with right and wrong, law must not contradict facts which have been established in an epistemologically sound way, that is, in accordance with the approved methodologies of scientific research and analysis. It must respect the truth because if it does not it cannot achieve *any* ends. The Clayton Act of 1914, for example, could not succeed because it contradicted economic truth in declaring that "the labor of a human being is not an article of commerce."

The function of law is to serve human aspiration in the broadest sense. If human aspiration is incompatible with reality, if it contradicts the laws of nature, of physics, chemistry, economics, or any other branch of knowledge, both humanity and law will fail. The law is failing today as an institution because the law schools and their products—lawyers, judges, legislators— have been too far out of touch with reality, not only the reality with which economics deals, but the realities of chemistry and physics and almost everything else as well.

I do not know whether Paul Poirot, my old and dear friend, will be happy with the conclusion I have reached, but just the same I dedicate this essay to him and to the years and the thoughts we have shared.

Professor Petro is the author of numerous books and articles on labor law and policy and other politico-economic matters. He is Director of The Institute for Law and Policy Analysis in Winston-Salem, North Carolina, and is a former FEE Trustee.

Child Labor and the British Industrial Revolution

BY LAWRENCE W. REED

EVERYONE agrees that in the 100 years between 1750 and 1850 there took place in Great Britain profound economic changes. This was the age of the Industrial Revolution, complete with a cascade of technical innovations, a vast increase in industrial production, a renaissance of world trade, and rapid growth of urban populations.

Where historians and other observers clash is in the interpretation of these great changes. Were they "good" or "bad"? Did they represent improvement to the citizens, or did these events set them back? Perhaps no other issue within this realm has generated more intellectual heat than the one concerning the labor of children. The enemies of freedom—of capitalism—have successfully cast this matter as an irrefutable indictment of the capitalist system as it was emerging in nineteenth-century Britain.

The many reports of poor working conditions and long hours of difficult toil make harrowing reading, to be sure. William Cooke Taylor wrote at the time about contemporary reformers who, witnessing children at work in factories, thought to themselves, "How much more delightful would have been the gambol of the free limbs on the hillside; the sight of the green mead with its spangles of buttercups and daisies; the song of the bird and the humming of the bee."[1]

Of those historians who have interpreted child labor in industrial Britain as a crime of capitalism, none have been more prominent than J. L. and Barbara Hammond. Their many works, including *Lord Shaftesbury, The Village Labourer, The Town Labourer,* and *The Skilled Labourer,* have been widely promoted as "authoritative" on the issue.

The Hammonds divided the factory children into two classes: "parish apprentice children" and "free labour children." It is a distinction of enormous significance, though one the authors themselves failed utterly to appreciate. Once having made the distinction, the Hammonds proceeded to treat the two classes as though no distinction between them existed at all. A deluge of false and misleading conclusions about capitalism and child labor has poured forth for years as a consequence.

Opportunity or Oppression?

"Free labour" children were those who lived at home but worked during the days in factories at the insistence of their parents or guardians. British historian E. P. Thompson, though generally critical of the factory system, nonetheless quite properly conceded that "it is perfectly true that the parents not only needed their children's earnings, but expected them to work."[2] Professor Ludwig von Mises, the great Austrian economist, put it well when he noted that the generally deplorable conditions extant for centuries before the Industrial Revolution, and the low levels of productivity which created them, *caused* families to embrace the new opportunities the factories represented:

> It is a distortion of facts to say that the factories carried off the housewives from the nurseries and the kitchen and the children from their play. These women had nothing to cook with and to feed their children. These children were destitute and starving. Their only refuge was the factory. It saved them, in the strict sense of the term, from death by starvation.[3]

Private factory owners could not forcibly subjugate "free labour" children; they could not compel them to work in conditions their parents found unacceptable. The mass exodus from the socialist Continent to increasingly capitalist, industrial Britain in the first half of the nineteenth century strongly suggests that people did indeed find the industrial order an attractive alternative. And no credible evidence exists which argues that parents in these early capitalist days were any less caring of their offspring than those of pre-capitalist times.

The situation, however, was much different for "parish apprentice" children, and close examination reveals that it was *these* children on whom the critics were focusing when they spoke of the "evils" of capitalism's Industrial Revolution. These youngsters, it turns out, were under the direct authority and supervision *not* of their parents in a free labor market, but of *government* officials. Most were orphans; a few were victims of negligent parents or parents whose health or lack of skills kept them from earning sufficient income to care for a family. All were in the custody of "parish authorities." As the Hammonds wrote,

> . . . the first mills were placed on streams, and the necessary labour was provided by the importation of cartloads of pauper children from the workhouses of the big towns. London was an important source, for since the passing of Hanway's Act in 1767 the child population in the workhouse had enormously increased, and the parish authorities were anxious to find relief from the burden of their mainte-nance . . . To the parish authorities, encumbered with great masses of unwanted children, the new cotton mills in Lancashire, Derby, and Notts were a godsend.[4]

The Hammonds proceed to report the horrors of these mills with descriptions like these: "crowded with overworked children," "hotbeds of putrid fever," "monotonous toil in a hell of human cruelty," and so forth. Page after page of the Hammonds' writings—as well as those of many other anticapitalist historians—deal in this manner with the condition of these parish apprentices. Though consigned to the control of a government authority, these children are routinely held up as victims of the "capitalist order."

Author Robert Hessen is one observer who has taken note of this historiographical mischief and has urged others to acknowledge the error. The parish apprentice children, he writes, "were sent into virtual slavery by *a government body*; they were deserted or orphaned pauper children who were legally under the custody of the poor-law officials in the parish, and who were bound by these officials into long terms of unpaid apprenticeship in return for bare subsistence."[5] Indeed, Hessen points out, the first Act in Britain which applied to factory children was passed to protect these very parish apprentices, not "free labour" children.

The Role of the State

It has not been uncommon for historians, including many who lived and wrote in the nineteenth century, to report the travails of the apprentice children without ever realizing they were effectively indicting *government*, not the economic arrangement of free exchange we call capitalism. In 1857, Alfred Kydd published a two-volume work entitled *The History of the Factory Movement*. He speaks of "living bodies caught in the iron grip of machinery in rapid motion, and whirled in the air, bones crushed, and blood cast copiously on the floor, because of physical exhaustion." Then, in a most revealing statement, in which he refers to the children's "owners," Kydd declares that "The factory apprentices have been *sold* (emphasis mine) by auction as 'bankrupt's effects.' "[6]

A surgeon by the name of Philip Gaskell made extensive observations of the physical condition of the manufacturing population in the 1830s. He published his findings in a book in 1836 entitled *Artisans and Machinery*. The casual reader would miss the fact that, in his revelations of ghastly conditions for children, he was referring to the parish apprentices:

> That glaring mismanagement existed in numberless instances there can be no doubt; and that these unprotected creatures, thus thrown entirely into the power of the manufacturer, were overworked, often badly-fed, and worse treated. No wonder can be felt that these glaring mischiefs attracted observation, and finally, led to the passing of the Apprentice Bill, a bill intended to regulate these matters.[7]

The Apprentice Bill that Gaskell mentioned was passed in 1802, the first of the much-heralded factory legislation, the very one Hessen stresses was aimed at the abuse by the parish officials. It remains that capitalism is not a system of compulsion. The lack of physical force, in fact, is what distinguishes it from pre-capitalist, feudal times. When feudalism reigned, men, women, and children were indeed "sold" at auction, forced to work long hours at arduous manual labor, and compelled to toil under whatever conditions and for whatever compensation pleased their masters. This was the system of serfdom, and the deplorable system of parish apprenticeship was a remnant of Britain's feudal past.

The emergence of capitalism was sparked by a desire of Englishmen to rid themselves of coercive economic arrangements. The free laborer increasingly supplanted the serf as capitalism blossomed. It is a gross and most unfortunate distortion of history for anyone to contend that capitalism or its industrialization was to blame for the agony of the apprentice children.

Though it is inaccurate to judge capitalism guilty of the sins of parish apprenticeship, it would also be inaccurate to assume that free labor children worked under ideal conditions in the early days of the Industrial Revolution. By today's standards, their situation was clearly bad. Such capitalist achievements as air conditioning and high levels of productivity would, in time, substantially ameliorate it, however. The evidence in favor of capitalism is thus compellingly suggestive: From 1750 to 1850, when the population of Great Britain nearly tripled, *the exclusive choice* of those flocking to the country for jobs was to work for private capitalists.

A discussion of child labor in Britain would be incomplete without some reference to the famous Sadler Report. Written by a member of Parliament in 1832 and filled with stories of brutality, degradation, and oppression against factory workers of all ages and status, it became the bible for indignant reformers well into the twentieth century. The Hammonds described it as "one of the main sources of our knowledge of the conditions of factory life at the time. Its pages bring before the reader in vivid form of dialogue the kind of life that was led by the victims of the new system."[8] Two other historians, B. L. Hutchins and A. Harrison, describe it as "one of the most valuable collections of evidence on industrial conditions that we possess."[9]

W. H. Hutt, in his essay, "The Factory System of the Early Nineteenth Century," reveals that bad as things were, they were never nearly as bad as the Sadler Report would have one believe. Sadler, it turns out, had been agitating for passage of the Ten Hours' Bill and in doing so he employed every cheap political trick in the book, including the falsification of evidence.[10] The report was part of those tactics.

Hutt quotes R. H. Greg (author of *The Factory Question*, 1837), who accused Sadler of giving to the world "such a mass of ex-parte statements, and of gross falsehoods and calumnies . . . as probably never before found their way into any public document."[11]

This view is shared by no less an anticapitalist than Friedrich Engels, partner of Karl Marx. In his book, *The Condition of the Working Class in England*, Engels says this of the Sadler Report:

> This is a very partisan document, which was drawn up entirely by enemies of the factory system for purely political purposes. Sadler was led astray by his passionate sympathies into making assertions of a most misleading and erroneous kind. He asked witnesses questions in such a way as to elicit answers which, although correct, nevertheless were stated in such a form as to give a wholly false impression.[12]

As already explained, the first of the factory legislation was an act of mercy for the enslaved apprentice children. Successive acts between 1819 and 1846, however, placed greater and greater restrictions on the employment of free labor children. Were they necessary to correct alleged "evils of industrialization"?

The evidence strongly suggests that whatever benefits the legislation may have produced by preventing children from going to work (or raising the cost of employing them) were marginal, and probably were outweighed by the harm the laws actually caused. Gaskell admitted a short time after one of them had passed that it "caused multitudes of children to be dismissed, but it has only increased the evils it was intended to remedy, and must of necessity be repealed."[13]

Hutt believes that "in the case of children's labor, the effects (of restrictive laws) went further than the mere loss of their work; they lost their training and, consequently, their skill as adults."[14]

Conditions of employment and sanitation were best, as the Factory Commission of 1833 documented, in the larger and newer factories. The owners of these larger establishments, which were more easily and frequently subject to visitation and scrutiny by inspectors, increasingly chose to dismiss children from employment rather than be subjected to elaborate, arbitrary, and ever-changing rules on how they might run a factory employing youths. The result of legislative intervention was that these dismissed children, most of whom needed to work in order to survive, were forced to seek jobs in smaller, older, and more out-of-the way places where sanitation, lighting, and safety were markedly inferior.[15] Those who could not find new jobs were reduced to the status of their counterparts a hundred years before, that is, to irregular and grueling agricultural labor, or worse—in the words of Mises—"infested the country as vagabonds, beggars, tramps, robbers, and prostitutes."[16]

So it is that child labor was relieved of its worst attributes not by legislative fiat, but by the progressive march of an ever more productive, capitalist system. Child labor was virtually eliminated when, for the first time in history, the productivity of parents in free labor markets rose to the point that it was no longer economically necessary for children to work in order to survive. The emancipators and benefactors of children were not legislators or factory inspectors, but factory owners and financiers. Their efforts and investments in machinery led to a rise in real wages, to a growing abundance of goods at lower prices, and to an incomparable improvement in the general standard of living.

Of all the interpretations of industrial history, it would be difficult to find one more perverse than that which ascribes the suffering of children to capitalism and its Industrial Revolution. The popular critique of child labor in industrial Britain is unwarranted, misdirected propaganda. The Hammonds and others should have focused on the activities of *government*, not capitalists, as the source of the children's plight. It is a confusion which has unnecessarily taken a heavy toll on the case for freedom and free markets. On this issue, it is long overdue for the friends of capitalism to take the ideological and historiographical offensive.

Professor Reed is Chief Economist for James U. Blanchard & Company in Jefferson, Louisiana, and is President of a public policy think tank in Midland, Michigan.

1. William Cooke Taylor, *The Factory System* (London, 1844), pp. 23–24.

2. E. P. Thompson, *The Making of the English Working Class* (New York: Random House, 1964), p. 339.

3. Ludwig von Mises, *Human Action* (New Haven, Connecticut: Yale University Press, 1949), p. 615.

4. J. L. and Barbara Hammond, *The Town Labourer* (New York: Augustus M. Kelley, 1967), p. 145.

5. Robert Hessen, "The Effects of the Industrial Revolution on Women and Children," in Ayn Rand, *Capitalism: The Unknown Ideal* (New York: New American Library, 1967), p. 112.

6. Alfred Kydd, *The History of the Factory Movement* (New York: Burt Franklin, n.d.), pp. 21–22.

7. Philip Gaskell, *Artisans and Machinery* (New York: Augustus M. Kelley, 1968), p. 141.

8. J. L. and Barbara Hammond, *Lord Shaftesbury* (London: Constable, 1933), p. 16.

9. B. L. Hutchins and A. Harrison, *A History of Factory Legislation* (New York: Augustus M. Kelley, 1966), p. 34.

10. W. H. Hutt, "The Factory System of the Early Nineteenth Century," in F. A. Hayek, *Capitalism and the Historians* (Chicago: University of Chicago Press, 1954), p. 1.

11. *Ibid.*

12. Friedrich Engels, *The Condition of the Working Class in England* (New York: The Macmillan Co., 1958), p. 192.

13. Gaskell, p. 67.

14. Hutt, p. 182.

15. Hessen, p. 112.

16. Mises, p. 614.

The Pen Is Mightier than the Plan

BY GREGORY F. REHMKE

FOR OVER three decades *The Freeman* has been a source of income for economists. *The Freeman* has purchased and published hundreds of short essays on topics ranging from the political economy of a campus hot dog stand to the causes of poverty in the underdeveloped world. For *The Freeman*, the proper role of economists is simply to teach economics. And the proper place for an economist is in front of a classroom of curious students, or seated quietly, pen in hand, before a blank sheet of paper (or, nowadays, keyboard in lap, before a blank computer monitor).

Freeman articles, however, have not been particularly popular with the majority of economists, perhaps because they have advocated a private property order that would not need economists advising government. A quiet satisfaction from explaining a concept, and a modest payment for thoughtful wordcraft are the rewards a free society would offer its economists.

What is this discipline that can be taught but not practiced? Economics is an apparatus of the mind, and economic concepts are tools of thought; they help us understand the daily flow of goods and services in a society. But economics is not a language of power or control; its concepts do not, in themselves, bestow power. Its concepts do not even provide management or investment expertise, and many a good economist has proved a poor investor or manager.

Yet, if *The Freeman*'s view of "economist as teacher" is reasonable, why are economists today among the most powerful men on earth; why do their reports and advice directly affect the lives of billions of people? One answer might be that some economists have succumbed to the allure of power and have, like wizards and astrologers before them, fashioned their advice to please those in power. Economists have come to advise kings, presidents, and prime ministers, have become the trusted counsel of congressmen and bureaucrats, judges and juries. Their brand of economic science claims to know what the most efficient role of government in society is. In the twentieth century economists have wedded "science" to political power.

No wonder *Freeman* articles have been so widely disregarded by the economic advisers on government payrolls. It is a sour message for a self-regarded scientist to hear that his science has, in practice, only power to destroy an economy, and that his proper role is to teach students how smoothly societies function without citizens understanding just how (and without needing to). The most important job for free market economists is, sadly, to try to undo the work of other economists.

While in North America economists have considerable influence in finance, industry, and government, in South America their influence has been even greater. From Mexico to Argentina, from Brazil to Peru, state by state, each capital has its priesthood of economists. Economists' sophisticated theories and well-researched studies have served to justify turning over ever larger control of Latin American resources to politicians and bureaucrats. The disaster of protectionism in Latin America finds its justification in works on "dependency theory" by top Latin American economists like Celso Furtado. His *Economic Development in Latin America* explains why protectionism is needed to escape from what he calls "traditional forms of external dependence." His reasons for keeping out foreign manufactured goods are the same as those Frederic Bastiat refuted in nineteenth-century France, when France tried to keep out English manufactured goods. As long as there are domestic manufacturers facing foreign competition there will be economists marketing "new" defenses of protectionism.

For decades economists served up their theory that modern economies were far too complex to be left unplanned, far too advanced to be left unsupervised. With foreign goods securely excluded, economists presented studies designed to "rationalize" economies. With such theories and studies as justification, hundreds of Latin American companies have been nationalized and most industries heavily regulated. Nationalization, economists argued, would help free their economies from foreign control and would keep future profits from leaving the country (though firms once nationalized generally stopped making profits altogether). Regulation, they said, would protect the consumer and prevent cutthroat competition and wasteful duplication.

With foreign competition locked out by protectionism, domestic competition was that much easier to suppress. Protectionism and regulation made the cartelization of domestic industry inevitable. The consequences of these policies have been disastrous. The lesson? Efficiency should never be a goal. The "creative destruction" of market capitalism never looks particularly efficient, often hiding productivity and progress in mountains of apparent waste from failed entrepreneurs and energetic competition. The market economy is a process and requires only a few rules to protect property, enforce contracts, and adjudicate torts.

But, economists said the government should do more, and claimed skills in fine tuning Latin American economies, skills in rearranging them and preparing them for bursts of growth. Enormous construction projects were advocated to speed development. The economist/planners must have known that much would be lost to waste and corruption as politicians made their modifications, and bureaucrats administered the details of the projects. They should have known that the politically connected builders would artfully revise and expand their cost-plus contracts. Yet there was, insisted the economists, no alternative: the economy must have development plans and development projects.

In Brazil, 360 major companies are owned and managed by the government, including four of the ten largest. Economists with university training in "public administration," "public finance," and "urban planning" advise these firms, while others run the bureaus that regulate companies in Brazil's private sector. In the political world, however, power shifts quickly to those most adept in its use. Though it was economists who provided the rationale for government ownership of private industry, and politicians who designed the laws to implement those theories, a third force has now risen to the top.

Influence and control have gravitated to a class of mixed-economy entrepreneurs, a breed of businessmen who flourish in mercantilism's mixture of commerce and privilege. As happened in the United States, regulatory agencies were quickly captured by the industries they were supposed to regulate. And, businessmen not adept in manipulating their regulatory agencies were soon outmaneuvered by their more adept (and often less principled) competitors.

Over time government-owned and -regulated firms become umbrellas providing for and protecting "families" of private sector suppliers and subcontractors—umbrellas wide enough to shield ever larger troops of unionized laborers, working ever shorter hours for ever more pay. The lucky few who made it into the government workers' unions learned, like their counterparts in management, to set their course by the stars of the developed world—and left their countrymen behind.

Hundreds of state-owned enterprises across Latin America pile up steady losses while steady profits flow to their politically connected "family" of dependent firms. When new technology or cheaper goods from foreign lands pose a threat, connected politicians and regulators are quick to come to the rescue, and quick to protect the status quo of the ancient regime. The YPF, Argentina's nationalized oil company, for example, loses $350 million a year, and even managed to lose money even during the oil boom of the 1970s. (David Asman, "Liberation Argentine Style," *Wall Street Journal*, May 4, 1987) But its private sector family of suppliers made fat profits selling overpriced parts, like perforation pipes, at twice world prices (after securing legislation that forced the YPF to buy domestic pipe, for which they are the only supplier). The state airline, Aerolineas Argentinas, loses $130 million a year, though its suppliers surely do well.

In his seven-month tenure as "Secretary of Growth Promotion" in Argentina, Manuel J. Tanoira found similar arrangements all across the Argentine economy. When Russian, German, and Argentine firms offered to take on a $300 million enlargement of Port Ingeniero White, the bureaucrats in charge avoided even formally receiving the proposals, much less considering them. The bureaucrats were waiting for IMF money to be promised so they could administer the project themselves, and divide the fat contracts among the local engineering and construction firms (and they know they will eventually turn to these same firms for future employment). (Manuel J. Tanoira, "Confessions of an Argentine Privatizer," *Wall Street Journal*, May 29, 1987, p. 27)

It was the same story for the toll roads private firms offered to build and pay for. Transportation bureaucrats at the *Vialidad Nacional* oppose all toll roads (and have even "liberated" some existing toll roads). Though they are able to block private construction of roads they seem unable to build any themselves. Their objection to toll roads is again a smokescreen for keeping the construction project and its lucrative contracts under their control.

Where Did the Idea Come From?

If we step back for a moment from the Third World horror stories, we wonder how it all could have happened. From where did the idea come that government should or could do anything beyond providing defense, a court system and police (and perhaps quietly mismanaging a postal service and a few lighthouses)? The vast intrusion of government into private sector development received theoretical support from a few key theories of "market failure."

Economists insisted that markets failed from time to time and that collective action, coercively funded, was a society's only hope. A modern economy ought to have a modern plan, and not be at the mercy of the "chaos of the market." Collectivization swept North America and Western Europe, but their wealthy economies and stable institutions had the wherewithal to survive until their governments eventually (and only partially) retreated from central planning. In Latin America the vogue of central planning, assisted by new international aid money, refueled the ancient mercantilist institutions that always cohabited their economies. Ironically, Spain of the sixteenth to nineteenth centuries avoided reforming its mercantilist institutions by ingesting a steady diet of gold and silver taken from Latin America. Now, in the second half of the twentieth century, Latin

America's own mercantilist institutions have survived only with the assistance of a similar infusion of wealth from Western banks and governments.

The private sector, market-failure theories explained, acts only in its narrow interests, so governments must design and carry out development plans (with the help of economic advisers, of course). Great hydroelectric dams were needed ("too large for private enterprise," claimed the economists) jungles needed taming ("roads and dams to provide the infrastructure to spur private sector development"); airports were needed, as were railroads, ports, and gleaming new capital cities perched on desolate plateaus. So it was theorized, so it was done; all these massive projects now stand in Latin America, along with thousands of smaller government-engineered cousins: neighborhood and village projects, office buildings, shopping malls, factories, and steel mills.

The economists, politicians, bureaucrats, and contractors have created much. From the rubble of the earth they have created a world where theories generate investigations that generate reports, followed eventually by projects that create jobs and provide services. All according to plan, but the plans have problems. Petrobras, for example, is Brazil's national oil company, and—not to be outdone by Argentina's YPF—engineered what *The Economist* cites as Brazil's biggest mistake in recent times. In the 1970s, just as the oil boom hit, Petrobras pulled back from oil exploration and poured its resources into alcohol and gasahol production. Alcohol is competitive at prices over $40 a barrel, but not below; so as Brazil's oil production stagnated (since its monopoly producer had put all its eggs in the alcohol basket), the bill from imported oil went from $280 million in 1970 to $10 billion in 1979. There was plenty of oil to be found in Brazil, but only now, after international prices have dropped dramatically, has the lumbering Petrobras been looking, finding, and producing. (*The Economist*, "Survey Brazil," April 25, 1987, p. 18)

Brazil's national road building program provides an example of how the best laid plans of economists get tweaked on their trek from theory to reality. Economists often complain that Third World countries lack sufficient infrastructure. They insist that though thousands of farms, ranches, and small industries would benefit from a connecting network of roads, the costs of organizing and financing such a system is beyond the means of the private sector. In Brazil the politicians agreed with their economic advisers that government roads were needed, and promptly financed a highway system connecting all but one of Brazil's state capitals. Most of these roads have little traffic, while new roads needed between commercial centers like Sao Paulo and Rio de Janeiro go unbuilt. He who pays the piper calls the tune.

The Polonoroeste plan, a project in the north of Brazil funded by the IMF, foreign lenders, and the government, was to develop some 100,000 square miles of tropical forest for small farmers. Some 17% of the land has been deforested so far. The farmers placed on small farms by the planners after the forests were slash burned are quickly going bankrupt on the thin jungle soil. Their exhausted land gets bought up and consolidated by cattle ranchers (who appeared nowhere on the original plans) (*Insight*, August 17, 1987, p. 16). Would the private sector have found it profitable to destroy thousands of square miles of jungle in order to provide cattle ranchers with inexpensive rangeland?

Brazilian planners and their economic advisers, like their counterparts across Latin America, have made mistakes. Many of the great projects built in Latin America over the past decades should not have been built, or at least should not have been built quite the way they were built. And it turns out that most of them have not been paid for. Creditors from overseas now want their money back—money spent by the billions in pursuit of a combined vision of economists and politicians that saw Latin America suddenly transformed into an industrialized and modernized civilization. Instead, Latin America has become a Frankenstein monster stitched together of ill-fitting pieces from the industrialized world, and, worst of all, sporting a head transplanted from mercantilist Europe of the sixteenth century.

Lately economists have been shifting gears. Now some proposals call for governments to sell off nationalized companies and deregulate their economies. Now, after billions of dollars, and millions of hours of labor have been lost in pursuit of these plans, after aching arms have welded miles of steel bars, poured sweat with uncounted tons of concrete into public projects across a hemisphere—they are blithely told their labor was lost, their capital squandered, their paychecks mere borrowings from foreign investors who will now and forever demand interest on the unpayable principal of those lost loans.

Instead of just accepting what economists say, perhaps economists should be taken out of the public-policy decision-making loop and returned to the profession of teaching. Latin America has had too much of economists. Too many failed economic plans, like Argentina's Austral plan and Brazil's Cruzado plan, darken the memories of once hopeful people. Too many failed projects litter Latin American landscapes—concrete and steel monuments to wasted resources and labor, symbols of a reach toward a modern world mysteriously never grasped, and ever-present reminders of self-esteem lost in the effort. Monuments, too, that are powerful magnets drawing wealth from Latin societies, pulling dollars through taxes, tariffs, and interest and exchange controls, to service debts incurred in their creation. A bad investment is no investment at all.

What New Vision for Latin America?

If *Freeman* authors were asked to advise Latin American governments, what advice would they offer? For starters they would suggest government officials get honest jobs in the private sector. Latin American governments need only get out of the way of their naturally entrepreneurial people. Entrepreneurship flourishes in Latin America's diverse underground economies, and these hard working people require only that their property rights be defined and defended and made freely transferable. They must be assured that their contracts are enforceable. They would like taxes drastically reduced and inflation stopped. And they would be most happy occasionally to read the thoughtful essays of their otherwise unoccupied economists in a journal much like *The Freeman*.

If such a revolution ever takes place in Latin America the role of economists in preserving it through education would perhaps redeem the profession for the evils wrought by its fallen associates.

Economist Alfredo Irigoin, in a recent letter to *The Wall Street Journal*, offered his thoughts on current plans for reform in Latin America proposed by American economists: "It is interesting to see how many intellectuals love to advocate policies for Latin America that they would not dare even to mention for the U.S. . . . Latin America does not need plans that call for more governmental interference, even when its ultimate goal is to establish a free-market order. Latin America needs a clearer definition of property rights to prevent governments from tinkering with the market, and a stable institutional framework to ignite entrepreneurial vision and alertness. Let the market choose—not the advisers." (*Wall Street Journal*, May 11, 1987)

One more time for emphasis: "Let the market choose—not the advisers"!

Mr. Rehmke is a member of the staff of The Foundation for Economic Education.

Why Liberty and Morality Are Inseparable

BY GEORGE C. ROCHE III

EXAMINING American culture today, one can find ample reason to despair of our future. On many sides we see the spread of false values and decadence. In too many places we see a dehumanizing impulse which cheapens the worth and dignity of life to the vanishing point. That impulse reveals a sickness in our underlying moral beliefs. Yet our headlong decline evokes only a murmur of concern and alarm. It is as if we were being fitted for our own annihilation.

"It is difficult to resist the conclusion," says Malcolm Muggeridge, "that Western man, having wearied of the struggle to be himself, has decided to abolish himself." He calls the contagion, with considerable justice, the "Great Liberal Death Wish." Whatever we call it, no one doubts we have terrible weapons to finish the job with deadly efficiency. But few notice we do it just as surely—if more slowly and more painfully—through starving the spirit. Man is the one creature on earth who cannot survive by the mere satisfaction of his animal appetites. Yet on the evidence, we seem concerned with little else.

In a generation's time we have inverted the ideals of all previous generations of Americans. We do not even understand our forefathers' words or goals. In these few years a tide of what may be called anti-heroism, centuries in the making, reached its flood-tide and inundated us. Many of us in our middle years have watched this tide and yet not known what we have seen. Thirty years ago we had no headline drug problem. Marijuana, cocaine, and the rest were relatively unknown. Crime rates were far lower and women could safely walk the streets in most areas. Abortions were rare, illegal, and to most, unthinkable. Taxes were less than a tenth what we pay now. First-class mail cost 3¢ and was delivered promptly. Coins were made of silver. Nobody worried about inflation. The "deficit" was not an issue; the government still had occasional surpluses. The few sleazy porn parlors around could not legally show a woman topless. Nowadays, to find something morally safe for your child to read, you head for a special "family" bookstore. And on the way you might drive by half a dozen "adult bookstores" peddling every kind of filth the mind can imagine. You see such now on the outskirts of even small towns, not long ago bulwarks of sane and sensible life.

I am not idealizing, much less conjuring up a happy childhood or fictions about the "good old days." Life always has its problems, but the change in recent years has been staggering.

It gives me no joy to review such cultural indices, to see how nearly we have squandered our estate. Heaven knows, I am no America-basher—that unctuous breed who positively relishes our every failing and distress, whose words salt and poison our wounds. (You know them: finger-pointers, cranks, sourpusses, tortured aesthetes, uglies, marchers, who demand that the world pay for their personal failure. Thoreau knew them: "If anything ails a man," he said, "so that he does not perform his functions if he have a pain in his bowel even, he forthwith sets about to reform the world." They are a large part of the problem at hand.) In truth, with the passing years, I love more than ever this fair land, its quiet homes, its untamed libertarian energy. Much of it remains unspoiled, and in many ways a finer, heroic spirit still moves us. Yet it must be admitted that we have changed and in the process have suffered a great loss. This is most plainly seen in the cultural decline which mirrors our faltering faith. Not until we isolate the pathogen can we attempt a cure. Otherwise, like a victim of fever, we will only slip deeper into lassitude, uncaring as the disease steals our waning strength.

Our affliction is specific. It is not as though, after two thousand years of contrary teaching, we have suddenly decided that sin is just the thing for more abundant life. The change was fostered and urged by a particular, anti-heroic view of reality. This view has historical origins in the West that can be traced. It is most readily understood (and derives its power) as a religion of Man, preaching a purely materialist interpretation of reality.

Anti-Heroism

Anti-heroism leaves clear fingerprints wherever it touches our culture. Among those fingerprints we should watch for assaults on, inversions of, weaseling about, and rationales for evading, traditional religious beliefs and a fixed transcendent standard of Good. The anti-hero does not believe in a personal God or in any spiritual purpose of men, and he finds numberless ways to say we are so many corks on the water, with no responsibility, individuality or value to our lives. Listen to all the television newscasters for a day, a week, a year. You will never hear them say the one straightforward thing: that today's horror was *wrong*, an evil act. Every other conceivable explanation will be trundled out, lest we admit evil. Society was to blame.

The terrorists were trying to dramatize their protest. The criminal came from a bad neighborhood. Only a psychotic would hack his mother into small pieces to collect the insurance.

Certain doctrines are equally revealing signatures of anti-heroism. Militant egalitarianism, for one: that obsessive urge all about us to deny all individuality and reduce everyone to "social units" of statistically identical condition. Wages are to be equalized, school classes leveled to the rate of the slowest child, the successful or rich humbled. Materialism, in the philosophic sense, is another signature. This is the claim that the things of this world are all there are, and it pretends to forget who is the "prince of the world." A collectivist bent is by its very nature anti-heroic. It is, indeed, a sign of the immaturity at the heart of all anti-heroic tenets. The anti-hero, like the adolescent, is the perpetual sucker for "group formation," and attributes mystical qualities to the group. "Peer pressure" and the voice of the mob reduce his guilty feelings about his acts. Like a child he thinks history began at his birth, and he cultivates a scorn for the past. Like a child he is sulky about accepting responsibility and dreams up ways to blame anybody, blame the whole world, for his own shortcomings.

The anti-heroic siege of Western values is comprehensive, and we could discuss it at almost any length. For example, look for an almost clinical aversion to suffering. The modern thinks the least discomfort is the curse of the fates and proof aplenty that there is no God, never suspecting that suffering is our greatest teacher. Look for an equal obsession with comfort, possessions and, most of all, sex. These are as close to happiness as the anti-hero can get, with sex the holy of holies. Never mind that children are abused or lethal diseases spread. Watch for the urge to lay bare all things, a tearing away of all veils of decency, an obscene (in the old sense) desire to see all in its seamy "natural" reality. Watch for the related "comradely" or Jacobin denial of manners, forms, tact, ritual, piety, ceremony: the inversion of civilized community. Watch for new expressions of the immoral formula, "the end justifies the means." Listen for adversion to science as the determinant of all truth, as if truth were bound to the material world which is the only world that science can investigate. Listen to the tireless moralizing by those who mind everybody's business but their own and will not speak of real good or evil. When you hear or see these things, you have found anti-heroes in their chosen calling of destroying the West.

For our predicament written large, just turn on the television—which we do on average, for something over forty hours per week. There we glaze our eyes and minds with the now proverbial sex and violence, car chases, and unending inanities. We drink in the "what is" of life in great draughts, neither asking for anything uplifting nor caring that we cannot find "what should be" in network programming.

The Plight of Education

The other great transmission belt of anti-heroism, directly to the young, and through them to the culture at large, is public education. As an educator, I see its product every day, even though the young people in my charge are, in the main, the sturdiest survivors of our secondary schools—the ones who, through family or religious influence, have fought their way clear.

The problem with our schools is not want of effort or money; we have long been lavish in those regards. We falter in having forgotten what education is. Albert J. Nock argued more than fifty years ago that education had vanished entirely from America. Malcolm Muggeridge snorts that "education" today is the great liberal poohbah, a "gigantic fraud" at public expense which seems almost intended to bring down civilization. The whole point of education is to pass along civilized and moral values from one generation to the next. What is now "taught" in many schools is the opposite—a smattering of facts and "subjects" as scrupulously free of values as the anti-hero can manage. And make no mistake, anti-heroes regard the schools as their own private preserve and demand monopolistic indoctrination in their own view. Anything other than uniform standards would be "undemocratic," you see. Meanwhile, huge bureaucracies are created to determine those standards.

Government at all levels is the purveyor of most education, and usually the worst. Degraded, anti-heroic curricula serve its purposes well and expand its power. Students trained in conformity and "adjustment" grow up to be compliant and docile taxpayers, neither mentally nor morally able to offer any resistance to growing state interventions. The state itself is the principal instrument of anti-heroism. The bloating of the federal government over the past fifty years is the most visible symptom of the anti-heroic penetration of American life. Having nothing to "render unto God," anti-heroes must perforce render all to Caesar. They are, to a man, all junkies of statism. In the absence of divine authority over men, the State, of necessity, becomes the final authority, taking on a quasi-divine—but far from benevolent—character. The apotheosis of the State to godhood is explicit in totalitarian regimes which war against all other religious observance ("Thou shalt have no other gods before me"). But all anti-heroic influence tends to the same end: the total State.

America was founded on exactly the opposite principle—another lesson taught falsely or omitted altogether in most school textbooks. The Founders agreed that government was at best a necessary evil, to be limited to a few specified functions by "the chains of the Constitution," and never to be trusted. The goal was maximal liberty and minimal state interference, a view presupposing that men are self-controlling, moral beings. The colonists had fought for their independence from onerous taxes and "a swarm" of the king's officers, with the slogans "Don't Tread on Me" and "Life, Liberty and Property." They meant to secure their liberties for all posterity with a limited, internally checked form of government and with the Constitution.

All this is gone, upended by anti-heroism in a virtual revolution. The greatest political changes, most agree, occurred in the Roosevelt years, beginning in 1933. But the real revolution began much earlier with the ascendancy of anti-heroic ideas, often imported from Europe. In the new view it is the individual person who is not to be trusted and the State that can do no wrong. It is as if we inverted the Jeffersonian maxim: "That government governs best which governs *most*"—no matter how bumbling, wasteful, boneheaded, bureaucratic, frustrating, bossy, and expensive its actions. The traditional relationships between the people and the State have been reversed. Where once government was conceived as the servant of the people, serving with their consent and at their sufferance, it has now become the master, and citizens are called "subjects." Cooperative society gives way to coercive rule. Equal opportunity for all in liberty surrenders to a massive maze of stolen legal privilege in the form of tax breaks, subsidies, tariffs, protectionism, legal monopolies, and so on. From a system rewarding diligence, prudence, and thrift, we turn to one of "income redistribution," penalizing effort and rewarding the most indolent, useless, and unproductive among us (bureaucrats very much included). Said the breathless ideologue of a century ago, when the State had absorbed all social energy, it would wither away. His legacy is the Superstate that is the most characteristic mark of the twentieth century. It is the individual who has withered away. We have become so many units for government statistics, so many income-producers to be taxed, so many subjects in bureaucratic dossiers.

Deluged by Politics

Accompanying this massive reversal of the American experiment in liberty has been a great politicization of our thinking and an almost berserk reference to "democracy." We are inundated with politics. Hardly a news item appears that is not couched in political overtones. It is the same story. Having, at anti-heroic urging, discarded any higher truth or authority over men, we necessarily turn all matters into political questions, to be settled by the councils and tribunals of men—preferably by counting heads. This elevates mere process to an absolute—another anti-heroic superstition. Follow the correct (democratic) procedure or formula, and never mind whether truth is served or the results are good. What follows is, in fact, very often atrocious: Hitler was elected, after all. But the anti-hero always has a high-sounding argument at hand, and he uses it constantly to justify his attacks on America's heritage and to conceal his loyalty to her enemies. But it is a cheat. His theories deny a genuine morality.

From a practical standpoint, Thomas Jefferson tried to warn us, the more government undertakes, the less it can perform its basic functions of keeping order, dispensing justice, and providing for the common defense. All of these are at present in disrepair. The anti-heroes are so busy inventing new "rights" that we forget the old and fundamental rights of life, liberty, and property, with which the new conflict. You cannot, for instance, declare a right to abortion at government expense without contravening both the baby's right to life and the taxpayer's right to keep what he earns. Such declarations are, to my mind, a none-too-subtle attack on our genuine rights. We spend more money on law enforcement every year, and the crime rate unfailingly goes up. We spend more money on education every year and the test scores unfailingly go down. What's going on here—other than the obvious fact that the government is the most bumbling performer we could turn to for either function? In Richard Weaver's words, "Ideas have consequences." The real deterrent to crime is moral law. We are to love our neighbor. We do not harm him: it is forbidden. We do not steal his property because it is in every sense his, the product of his effort, and in no way ours. No man of self-respect would touch what does not belong to him.

Before we take leave of the rude, anti-heroic intrusions of government, we must note its greatest effrontery: its trampling of the whole concept of justice. According to three thousand years of Greek, Judaic, Roman, and Christian teaching, justice means "to each his due," equality before the law. About a hundred years ago at Harvard Law School, then as now in the vanguard of anti-heroism, the good professors decided that what was important was winning the case, not justice. And there began an avalanche of injustice.

It has long since become routine for lawyers to use delays and legal trickery to gain acquittal for crooks they know full well are guilty. This practice is defended not only as permissible but "ethical": in the name of providing the "best possible" defense. But the tactics employed can be ethically questionable or worse, and the end served is the defeat of justice. This process has been abetted by a long series of court decisions establishing a wide array of ultra-finicky procedural "rights" for the accused. Let the police or prosecutor make the slightest error, and all the evidence in an otherwise open-and-shut case can be thrown out, and a criminal freed. Thus justice is subverted by the "winning is everything" doctrine, an anti-heroic formula. Under it criminal activity becomes more profitable and crime rates climb.

But that's just the start. Having bitten the apple, the legal profession and "public interest" groups have in recent years engineered what has been called the "tort revolution." What it amounts to is a system of legal theft, aimed at the rich, but affecting us all by making fault irrelevant in most liability suits.

Hostility to free markets is also a general and clear signature of anti-heroism. This, in part, reflects the lingering effects of Marx's primitive "economic theories"—if they may be so dignified. These were so crude as to be demonstrably false before the ink was dry, and embarrassed even socialists. (Some future student will find Marx's flighty assumptions, abstractions, and tortuous arguments the very model of anti-heroic thinking—the sort of thing that led Marx to insist wages must fall to subsistence levels smack in the middle of a century of rapidly rising wages.) However absurd the theory, all its prejudicial conclusions were retained and are still widely expressed in hatred for, and attacks on, a free economic order, i.e., "capitalism."

In another sense, Marxist theory did not and does not matter. Its real purpose was to turn envy into righteousness and to justify the immemorial resentments of weaklings and failures toward more successful men. In envy, Marx's followers already clung to the ancient fallacy that "wealth" was static, not constantly created. It follows from this blunder—despite the fact that it had been exploded by Adam Smith a century earlier, in *Wealth of Nations* (1776)—that to acquire wealth you had to *steal* it from somebody else. All they wanted was an excuse to unleash their envy and hatred with moral righteousness, and Marx gave it to them: "capitalism is theft." With this they could claim justice while revenging themselves on their "bourgeois oppressors" with merciless class war and extermination. No demonstration in this century has been more overwhelming than the folly and brutality of such thinking on the one hand when compared with the moral and economic superiority of free markets on the other. Yet the anti-hero nurses his old fallacies and false righteousness to vent his grudges against "the rich." Deep down he says, "It's not my fault I am not more successful. It's theirs, it's the system's, it's the world's." Deeming himself to be sensitive and superior, he reasons that if the world does not recognize it, the world is not good enough for him. He will punish it. If the system doesn't put him at the top of the heap, nobody else can be, either. He will level it. If he is not financially successful, he will turn up his nose at "grubby materialistic commerce." If he inherits wealth, he is commonly filled with guilt, and often uses his money to advance "the cause." He gravitates naturally to bureaucratic or tenured academic positions, where advancement is by seniority and success is not measured in dollars. There he can nurse his brooding grudges and form cliques with others of like mind, to get mutual support and to rail against the injustice of it all. From this cesspool of whiny self-justifications, anti-heroic posturing, and venomous envies springs the modern's loathing for free markets in a free society. America, symbol of freedom and success, is for that very reason the quintessence of evil in the eyes of the anti-heroic intellectual—here as well as abroad. We do not understand anti-heroism adequately until we see its roots in envy and its motivation in revenge.

Nobel laureate Milton Friedman has remarked that "all interventions [in the market] are counterproductive." This is true, and once it might have alerted us to the cost of political meddling: it could harm our standard of living. This is no longer enough. The ascendancy of anti-heroism, especially in the last two decades, has lulled us into believing that our vaunted standard of living is all there is, and that a perpetually rising Gross National Product is our promise of heaven on earth. In this we forget our higher purposes in life, and make ourselves accomplices in our own execution. The anti-hero knows, if only instinctively, what we are forgetting, that the marketplace has more and higher purposes than money grubbing. Markets reflect our spiritual values as well as our free economic choices. They are a bulwark of life, liberty, and what Weaver called "the last metaphysical right," property. If in nothing else, we can at least see that economic freedom gives us the surplus we need for charity and philanthropy, for caring for the needy, for building synagogues and churches. We err greatly in separating things into neat little categories: commerce here, charity there. As Ludwig von Mises showed, they are all part of an interlocking system of free choice. Recent scholarship by George Gilder and others has established the moral and altruistic basis of entrepreneurial capitalism. Lord Acton used to be fond of saying that the tenets of modern economics could all be found in the Gospel. We have always been able to *see* the difference: not only the obvious economic superiority but the moral health on this side of the Iron Curtain.

Restoring the Heroic in Our Lives

Unfortunately, the anti-hero is especially crafty in persuading us that money, not morality, is all there is to markets. That opens every door to his attack. Heavens! He does not want to kill the goose, no sir. He just wants to regulate the market, tame it, tax it, suppress "greed," prevent "fraud," stop pollution, correct market inefficiencies, and blah blah. We've all heard it. And in his sway we think, "he's just fine-tuning; let the experts keep the GNP rising, do the planning, improve our standard of living." But he is destroying our markets, our freedom and, what matters more, our moral capacities. The economy is not a "thing"; it is ourselves exercising our free and moral choices. Markets—"people power"—are strong and resilient, but cannot withstand indefinitely an anti-heroic siege that brings grafters and politicians into the service of anti-heroic ideologues, do-gooders, and "public interest" busybodies. We have lost a sizable fraction of our freedom and rights to this weird coalition, and notwithstanding a few successes with deregulation of late, stand to lose much more—or all. There's nothing between us and Soviet-style bread lines except restoration of the heroic, religious basis of life.

We must, in short, keep our balance between the worldly and spiritual sides of our nature. The former, carried to its extreme, its *reductio ad absurdum*, by anti-heroism, produces what I think is the ultimate temerity of the modern world: central economic planning. It sounds so cool and scientific and rational that we are easily seduced by the idea. But what it amounts to is the imposition by force of the notions of a few government whizzes in place of and overruling the infinitely better informed choices of all of us in the market, each of us informed by our own circumstances and ever-changing scale of virtues and preferences. The presumption that the central planner can do better for us than millions of us can do for ourselves is monstrous. Our "unplanned" open market is the reason our stores overflow with luxuries while workers stand in line for necessities in anti-heroic utopias.

With what incredible gall, then, are we to claim to "plan" the doings of that most complex creature, moral man? In this regard, "I have an earnest proposal to make," said the biologist Lewis Thomas. "I suggest that we defer further action until we have acquired a really complete set of information concerning at least one living thing. Then, at least, we shall be able to claim that we know what we are doing." For that simple organism, anyway. "The delay might take a decade; let us say a decade. We, and the other nations, might set it as an objective of international, collaborative science to achieve a complete understanding of a single form of life. . . . As to the subject, I propose a simple one, easily solved within ten years. It is the protozoan *Myxotrichia paradoxa*, which inhabits the inner reaches of the digestive tract of Australian termites." The idea, of course, went nowhere, and we still know little about *M. paradoxa*. But the anti-hero, in conscience-less cruelty, goes on advocating more creative "five-year plans" to dictate the lives of all.

But it takes nothing more than waking up to end a nightmare. Our bad dream will end as soon as we see what it is. I believe that it is already ending, and that the worst is behind us. but we are barely past the crest of the anti-heroic tide. There is much peril before us, and much to do.

We Americans have always known something the world sometimes forgets: that the right tree bears the good fruit. We can judge anything by results. If our machine doesn't work, we know we botched the design. If we put water in the gas tank, we know that's why our car doesn't run. The same for the philosophic schemes of men. If the results don't live up to the promise; if we are not happier and morally healthier for them, we *know* beyond any doubt they are wrong.

We still have a choice. Anti-heroism has no irresistible claim on us. We can dump the whole reeking works over the cliff with no more than a decision to do so. Its claim to make a full and true accounting of the whole cosmos is just ludicrous. It is literal madness. It is our best scientists who tell us how little we know of even the material world science can study. It is our wiser philosophers who remind us how little we have unraveled of the mysteries of life. Who, but the anti-hero, is so presumptuous and proud as to press a claim for governorship of the whole cosmos when we cannot govern nations or even ourselves?

Let's use our American sense. It is anti-heroism that flunks the test of truth. If it could have made us happier and better, it would have long before now. Instead it makes us miserable. If it were true, it would always have been true. There could never have been any dispute about our way of life at all, nor any arguments against it to beguile us today. We would always have been what the anti-hero says we are now, mere beasts of the field, more intelligent than the others perhaps, but literally unable to do or see more than beasts can do or see. We would never have had any great literature or art, not to mention entrepreneurial success. There would never have been such a thing as America. The nature of reality has not changed. We have changed, because we have been suckered: and we can change right back again by seeing through the lies and saying no to them. Or we can sink deeper into the come-lately grunts of the world. The one thing no man can do is stand aside.

These collected essays are written with affection and respect for one man who has chosen not to stand aside. In a long career at The Foundation for Economic Education, Paul Poirot has consistently reflected the values, the dignity and the commitment to individual freedom which must be defended if we are to restore this country and this civilization. No one knows better than Paul Poirot what the stakes are in the battle, and none has fought harder for those things in which we all believe.

Dr. Roche is President of Hillsdale College, Hillsdale, Michigan. He was Director of Seminars at The Foundation for Economic Education from 1966 to 1971 and is currently a member of FEE's Board of Trustees.

Make-Work Jobs

BY DEAN RUSSELL

THE IDEA that "government should provide a job for any person who wants to work, and can't find employment" became a permanent part of the American economic philosophy during the terrible depression of the 1930s. Over the years, that idea has developed from "a job of any kind, however undesirable and low-paying" into the idea of "a meaningful job at an acceptable rate of pay."

But as is *always* the case when our government interferes in the market place, there are unforeseen "neighborhood effects." And as often as not, these unanticipated consequences are destructive of the very persons the programs were designed to help. The *Comprehensive Employment and Training Act* (CETA, a program to help disadvantaged people get jobs) is an excellent example of these government programs in action.

When CETA was proudly launched in 1975, it was announced as a program to bring order to the sprawling field of government job-training activities that had cost us taxpayers hundreds of billions of dollars over the past 25 years. I suppose our congressmen were getting tired of being reminded that unemployment was increasing (not decreasing) as these government make-work projects continued to expand and grow.

From 1975 to 1982 (the first eight years of CETA), the government agency "spent over $60 billion. . . . but the unemployment rate is higher now than when it started." (*Policy Review*, Spring, 1983) The unemployment rate climbed steadily, even though "Local governments began openly subsidizing payrolls with CETA money to the point where 15–25–30 percent and more of their employees are now drawing Federal paychecks. . . . David Meiselman notes in a penetrating study of public-sector jobs, 'more unemployment results as workers wait longer and search longer for preferred public-sector jobs rather than take private-sector jobs.' " (*The Reader's Digest*, August 1978)

But the unforgivable result of that program is this: "CETA has become

. . . a fraud . . . on the disadvantaged people whose hopes for lasting, useful employment it has falsely raised." (*Digest*, above.)

We're all now pretty well inured to the wasting of billions of tax dollars by the government; it's so commonplace it's just not news anymore. But to raise the expectations (and then destroy the hopes) of human beings is just not nice.

Here's how I personally got involved in what turned out to be the "wasting" of one more human being through CETA and its claim to help people who are "educationally handicapped." Apparently that's a euphemism to identify those who can't get jobs because they have no job skills; so why not use the taxpayers' money to train them so they can get and keep jobs? Sounds logical enough, and even charitable. And no one can seriously argue with the idea that it's more expensive to pay persons to stay on welfare forever than it is to pay for a program to train them to perform useful jobs. So (presuming that the government is going to do one or the other), the CETA approach appears to be more logical than most social programs by government.

My university agreed to participate in the CETA program. My department was asked to provide a job for one CETA employee, who had already been trained as a typist/filing clerk in another government program. We were told that the hiring of this employee would cost us nothing. I was appointed to "look into it" and to make a recommendation to my fellow professors.

I discovered that, while we had no budget for an additional typist/filing clerk, most of us professors were more than willing to have a private typist instead of sharing the three in the departmental "pool." So there was no problem in finding a place for her. In fact, the competition for her services became so keen that we soon decided just to add her to the pool, where her services would be available to all.

Then I discovered that the Federal salary guarantee was for one year only. After that, we were supposed to fit her into our regular budget. But that was already set for the next two years. So at the end of the year, our choices would be to "let her go," or keep her and fire one of the three regular civil-service-protected typists (fat chance), or to allocate a large chunk of our "travel money" to pay her salary (also, fat chance), or to cut our budget for office supplies, and so on. No one was willing to make the needed sacrifice to pay for the unneeded job we were creating. So I finally recommended that we decline the Federal offer of a free typist.

I was overruled; my colleagues were simply appalled at my heartlessness. "After all, she needs the job." So the young lady came aboard. She could type but not well. She could file, but only under supervision. She was indeed "educationally handicapped" and truly needed help, which we all gave her as best we could.

The end of the year came. Since there was no money to pay her, it seemed she'd lose her job. But as I had anticipated all along, that proved to be awkward if not impossible. She liked her job "working with the fine people at the university." And after all, "You did hire me, you know." Expectations.

We eventually found the money in one of the administrative budgets to pay her for another year; after that, we hoped to work her job into our regular budget. The "recession" of the early 1980s appeared. Not only did we get no increase in our budget, but it was actually cut by three percent. There wasn't even a raise for us professors. (Now that just won't do, not at all.)

Thus the CETA typist had to be fired. I believe the preferred academic euphemism is, "Her contract was non-renewed." Whichever, she lost her job.

There were tears, of course. But that wasn't nearly as shattering as her look of total incomprehension. I felt terrible. We had led her to believe she had a real job when it was only a make-work job. She was bitter, as she had every right to be. The learned explanations made to her by my learned colleagues were not helpful. In fact, I suspect I was the only person who really listened to them. I just wanted to see if they, themselves, had any comprehension of what had happened, and especially why. In essence, most of them merely said, "The government should do something about this sad case."

I didn't bother to tell them it *was* the government (egged on by us do-gooders who were sincerely trying to help) that had created this disastrous situation that was about to destroy another human being. If I were to try to tell them, I'd only get looks of incomprehension—plus puzzled stares at a "cold-hearted colleague who would let people lose their jobs and starve."

Dr. Russell is a writer and retired college professor. He was a member of the FEE staff during the 1950s.

Eternal Hope

by Hans F. Sennholz

WE are never beneath hope; in all things it is better to hope than to despair. In the political world much can be done if man changes his mind and brings a thorough will to do it. There is no inevitability in the coming of inflation, deflation, or regimentation. Man makes laws and repeals them. He has made laws that are sowing the seeds of conflict and strife; he can repeal them. He has enacted laws that are promising to do what laws cannot do; he can rescind them. Man may live above his circumstances or decide to live within his means. He may indulge in deficit spending or balance his budget; there are no uncontrollable expenditures, no unavoidable deficits.

He who reforms himself is doing much to reform others. Reform, like charity, must begin at home. Once accomplished at home, it will radiate outward, kindle new light, and ever spread in geometric proportion. The true reformer is a seminal reformer, not a radical. He does not pass laws that mandate the reformation of others. He himself makes a beginning and does not think of himself as a reformer. The world may reject him as odd, impractical, and even irrational; but he clings to his principles regardless of the world around him. There is boldness, a spirit of daring in the heart of a reformer.

Significant reforms, in final analysis, are moral reforms, changes in the perception of right conduct. Certain moral standards are basic to the social order: sanctity of human life and dignity of the individual; they may not change much from one generation to the next. Other standards may undergo visible changes in the span of one generation or two, such as individual independence and self-reliance, the ethos of labor and thrift, honesty and integrity, respect for private property. Changes in these standards lead to changes in the system of economic and social organization. In this century they sowed the seeds of economic and social conflict and paved the way for political intervention in our lives. They gave birth to a transfer and entitlement system that is eroding the private property order. A reform that would restore it and remove the transfer predilection would have to restore the harmony of interests and repair the moral standards. It would have to rebuild the economic order on the old foundation of the eighth Commandment—*Thou shalt not steal*—and of the tenth—*Thou shalt not covet anything that is thy neighbor's.*

Breaching the Strongholds

To reconstruct a moral order is to set shining examples in the very strongholds of the political transfer system.[1] Reconstruction would have to begin with Social Security and Medicare, the most expensive and imposing bastions of the system, formidable and intimidating to all reformers. They are the very pillars of the transfer system; to exempt them from review and render them untouchable is to leave the system untouched. To exempt them from budget restraint when massive deficits are suffered and other programs are cut, is to reaffirm the very transfer system. The Reagan Administration reconfirmed the Roosevelt Social Security system and the Johnson Medicare system when it not only rendered them untouchable and uncontrollable, but also reinforced them with "catastrophic insurance" and "nursing care."

It is difficult to castigate the transfer system with economic arguments. Surely, economists can point out that political transfer breeds economic and social conflict, that it reduces labor productivity and income, and that, in the end, it weakens and impoverishes the transfer society. All these effects are subject to explanation and interpretation; the causes can be explained away and the effects may actually be used to justify ever more political transfer. Growing poverty may bring forth ever more government intervention seeking to alleviate poverty. Moreover, economic arguments deploring "lack of funds" and "red-ink spending" are likely to be counterproductive. To point at empty pockets and treasuries in the sight of much wealth and luxury all around us does not ring true. It is utterly ineffective against passionate descriptions of human need and want. Yet, the most common criticism leveled at the transfer system is "we cannot afford it." It leaves the moral argument for transfer and entitlement completely unanswered; instead, it initiates a search for funds that make it affordable. In the end, the funds are promptly secured through higher taxes on young people or deficit financing that consumes their savings.

Social Security

It is futile to point at the costs of the Social Security System. Today, 126 million workers (more than 9 out of 10) pay more than $227 billion a year so that some 40 million retired or disabled people and their dependents may receive monthly Social Security checks. They pay more than $82 billion so that over 23 million people, 65 and over, nearly all of the nation's older population, draw healthcare benefits under Medicare; another 3 million disabled people under 65 enjoy the same benefits. Obviously, every American has a stake in Social Security, either as a beneficiary or a victim, or both.[2]

It is a formidable system built on political expedience and political immorality. It exacts income and wealth from one social class in order to enrich another. It keeps on growing and shifting an ever-growing burden on the working people. Sooner or later the victims may resent the shifting and endeavor to lighten their load through realistic reductions in benefits or outright repudiation. They may want to abolish the System because it is the product of politics, very popular with politicians and their beneficiaries, and yet so grossly unjust and unethical. The reform generation may want to halt the feverish efforts at transfer and liquidate the System proceeding along the following lines:[3]

Information to Recipients. To restore a commonplace truth and realism, every recipient of Social Security benefits should be informed of the nature and source of his benefits. Every check should carry a stub that reveals the dollar amount contributed to the System by him and his employer and the cumulative amount of benefits received by him as of that check. The stub should show that he or she contributed a total of $817.15 and as of now has withdrawn $69,501.15. Such shocking revelation would soon silence the most common defense: "I paid in."

Means Test. When the total benefits received in retirement exceed the contributions made during the productive years, the recipient should undergo a means test. Anyone who can cover his own expenses should be expected to do so. Millionaires and other affluent retirees should be expected to pay their own bills. A poor retiree who is lacking the means of support may seek public assistance. He is getting it now, but calling it "Social Security."

Parent and Child. When public assistance seems to be called for, the children of a retired worker should be given an opportunity to contribute to the support of their parents. As the parents are responsible for their children, so are children responsible for their parents. No Social Security System should eradicate this moral law and Biblical Commandment.

Conscientious Objectors. The System should not violate the religious and moral principles of conscientious objectors. Even in such a vital matter as national defense, American society has always respected the principles of those Americans who refused to bear arms or participate in military service. The same respect should be accorded to all religious and moral objectors to Social Security.

Relief for Young Workers. To grant relief to the primary victims of the System and abate the frantic shifting of burdens to future generations, we should seek to protect our youth by limiting its losses. To this end it is proposed that no one should be forced to remain in the System. Anyone willing to assume self-responsibility for his old age and his medical expenses should be permitted to do so.

The financial dilemma of the Social Security System is giving rise to numerous reform proposals. Many turn out to be new concoctions of the same old redistribution medicine, prescribing new victims for old beneficiaries. In contrast, these proposals begin with truth and information, which are the seeds for a true reform, and build on moral conduct rather than political expedience. Reformation is a work of time. We must rebuild and regenerate moral awareness which in time will bring forth genuine reform.

Medicare

In the meantime, it is time to brace ourselves for another financial crisis: the crisis of Medicare.[4] When the U.S. Congress is not coping with Social Security losses it is struggling with Medicare deficits. Just recently it was facing staggering Social Security deficits that were estimated at $180 billion over a seven-year period; now the budget office is warning us of a $310 billion accumulated Medicare deficit by 1995. It is clear that the Health Insurance Fund is in serious financial trouble. In fact, it is facing insolvency within four years unless Congress finds a way to raise revenue or control soaring medical expenditures.

The dilemma of Medicare is a dangerous political issue. At any moment it may explode into a partisan fracas such as the bitter confrontations on Social Security. Vying for the votes of the elderly, the political parties may again accuse each other of callous disregard of decency, responsibility, and morality. Surely, in the end they can be expected to cooperate again by raising the tax levies on some hapless taxpayers. The question of morality then will be shelved until such time when Medicare needs to be rescued again.

To many observers, Medicare is an unfailing index of political immorality. Born from the transfer entitlement mentality in the 1960s, fostered by political power and government force, nourished by tax collectors and IRS agents, Medicare is a creature of politics. It takes income and wealth from some people in order to finance the medical bills of other people. It rests on brute political force that uses the instruments of government to benefit one social class at the expense of other classes.

According to all financial analyses, the distribution of personal wealth is directly proportional to the age of the individual. Young people as a class are much poorer than old people, most of whom managed to accumulate some measure of material comfort and wealth. Unfortunately, transfer policies are rarely guided by considerations of comfort and wealth; they are determined by political power and popular majority, which places youth at a distinct disadvantage in the political process. The elderly manage to vote themselves benefit entitlements and allocate the costs to younger people.

They work through Medicare which seizes income and wealth from the poorer classes and bestows free medical benefits on their own.

The very existence of Medicare raises difficult questions of political morality. Is it moral for a political majority to seize income and wealth from one social class, in this case the younger poorer population, in order to benefit another social class? Is it right to use the apparatus of government to benefit one social class at the expense of others? Is it proper and just to establish permanent transfer agencies that redistribute income and wealth?

The moral question of Medicare raises many questions of individual conscience and behavior. Is it proper, fair, and moral for an individual to partake of the transfer benefits derived by political force? Someone's Medicare benefit is always a painful financial exaction from someone else. Is it moral for anyone to inflict such pains on others? In particular, the dear old lady in mink and a six-figure bank account, is she acting morally when she inflicts the Medicare pains on young people by claiming her benefits? The Medicare card in the pocket of an heiress to the Rockefeller, Ford, or Mellon fortunes, is it not a glaring badge of political immorality? Is it not such a badge in anyone's pocket?

What are we to think of an affluent family whose aging mother depends for her medical needs on government and Medicare? What are we to think of sons and daughters who deliver their parents to Medicare? How are we to judge a Medicare society?

We may not find fault with the doctor who serves Medicare patients unless he becomes a spokesman and promoter of the system. After all, a doctor who is providing health care services to the sick and needy cannot be expected to search into the sources of the money he receives in exchange. He may even specialize in and concentrate on services rendered to Medicare patients because there is a profitable demand. And yet, he should not be faulted as long as he does not promote it, he himself does not use it, or urge his mother to use it. We may even applaud him when he reminds the dear-old-lady patient in mink of the poor taxpayers who are forced to pay her bills.

Many critics of the Medicare system are questioning its medical effectiveness and cost efficiency. They are lamenting the health-cost inflation and are searching for solutions. They rarely raise the crucial question of political morality. Should an immoral system be made more effective and cost-efficient? Or should it be reformed along the lines of Judeo-Christian morality? Can the cost issue ever be resolved without first solving the moral issue?

The federal government must be extricated from the health care business. To allow politicians and bureaucrats in any business is to inject political immorality. After all, most politicians make decisions on the basis of popular majority rather than given morality. They take polls rather than reflect on basic principles of morality. Unfortunately, opinion polls provide no guidepost for questions of morality.

Medicare reformers are concerned about the special interests in the health care industry that make it the special target of politics. Surely, in the lives of most people, food, clothing, and shelter are more important than medical care. Most of the time they are more important also in the lives of the elderly. To sustain human life the farmer, butcher, baker, textile worker, carpenter, plumber, and many others are as indispensable as the doctor and nurse. Why then should the former be taxed so that the latter be subsidized? Why should health care of the elderly be singled out and be regulated and controlled by politicians?

Medicare critics applaud anyone's effort to force Medicare cuts through Congress. They favor all efforts to trim costs by raising premiums and "co-payments," the share of the health care burden borne by Medicare recipients. In particular, they are demanding a "means test" that would eliminate the most glaring cases of political immorality, the Medicare cards issued to millionaires and billionaires, and all others who are more able to pay their medical bills than young people. They would extend the means test also to the children of the elderly claiming Medicare and Medicaid benefits. Why should affluent sons and daughters not be expected to cover the medical bills of their needy parents?

When children abandon the care of their parents to government and its institutions, both suffer tragic losses. Most of all, the children lose their possibility of growth in being human and moral. And in days to come, their iniquities will be visited upon them as their children imitate them.

What the critics of the system are unable to accomplish through information and education, the AIDS virus may achieve in less than a decade.[5] It is devastating the government health care system. Some three to four million Americans are presently infected by the dread disease, and every ten to twelve months the number of AIDS patients is doubling. If it continues to double every year, 64 million Americans are estimated to be infected by the end of 1990, just three years from now. Health officials expect that one million patients will soon die every year, and ten million in 2000. With just 1,260,000 hospital beds available in the U.S., the hospitals are likely to be crowded. At the present, AIDS patients are staying an average of 167 days in the hospital before they die, at an expense of some $147,000 per patient. In the year 2000, if no cure is found, it will take nearly $1.5 trillion to nurse them until they die.

The immoral transfer system places the financial burden on Medicare and Medicaid. The dying call out for Medicaid to bear their medical expenses; the survivors of the deceased who worked under Social Security for at least 1 1/2 years in the 3 years before death, qualify for Social Security survivor benefits. No matter what dollar amounts the system may exact from its working people, the revenue will be grossly insufficient to cover the AIDS health care demand.

In ages gone, when moral obligation meant conformity to the will of God, carriers of contagious diseases who knowingly and willfully infected other individuals and thereby inflicted great suffering and early death on others, would have been treated as criminals, yea, even as murderers, and been promptly quarantined from the healthy community. The transfer society, in contrast, is jealously safeguarding the civil rights of AIDS carriers who may infect others with criminal immunity; it is eagerly loading the financial burden of their care on working survivors, and squarely placing politicians and officials in charge of it all. A mysterious death wish seems to drive the transfer society; the AIDS epidemic may make it come true.

A Spending Freeze

The critics of the transfer order draw an important distinction between political intervention that is continuously misdirecting economic activity and hampering economic production, such as all forms of price and wage controls, and that intervention which benefits one class of people at the expense of another. The former must be abolished without delay, the latter in an orderly fashion.

The strongholds of the American transfer system, Social Security and Medicare, must be dismantled in an orderly fashion. The beneficiaries must be made aware of the nature of their benefits and be placed on notice that the transfer process will be terminated. The first step in this direction must be a spending freeze that calls a truce to the political struggle.

In reaction to popular criticism, a few politicians have made deficit reduction proposals and even urged spending freezes in order to meet certain deficit targets. Spending does not need to be cut, taxes need not be raised, they inform us; expenditures must be frozen until the natural growth in revenues catches up with the spending. If expenditures are kept constant for a while, the budget deficit will shrink and eventually disappear.

Senator Pete Domenici of New Mexico recently proposed that Congress freeze Fiscal Year 1988 budget authority at Fiscal Year 1987 spending levels.[6] Federal spending in 1987 is estimated at $1 trillion, revenues at $850 billion. Revenues are estimated to rise to $933 in FY 1988, to $996 in 1989, and $1.058 trillion in 1990.[7] If expenditures were frozen at 1987 levels until 1990, the Federal budget would be in the black.

The Domenici proposal, like so many other deficit reduction proposals, attacks the symptoms instead of the disease. Surely, it points at the high growth rate of spending and urges temporary moderation until receipts catch up with outlays. Unfortunately, it does not in the least touch upon the root cause of the evil, the transfer mentality, which generates outlays faster than revenue can be collected. The Domenici proposal holds out new hope for more benefits in 1990 when surpluses would be expected. While it deplores the red ink it implicitly welcomes the transfer accounts.

It is significant that the Domenici freeze would exempt government pay increases and Congressional salary raises. If it is true that example is more forcible than precept, the Domenici exemption is likely to be more persuasive than the proposal. To an outside observer, political objectives present inscrutable puzzles of intent, design, and sincerity.

A New Beginning

A world is a scene of changes. Conditions will either get better or grow worse; they are unlikely to remain the same for long. Pessimists who instinctively take the gloomiest possible view of a situation are holding to the belief that all things ultimately tend toward evil. They are preparing for ever larger fiscal debts and deficits, followed by soaring inflation and deteriorating levels of living. They are convinced that a society that is preoccupied with entitlement and depredation cannot remain free for long. Pessimists take a dim view of optimists who, observing the present trend, may not deny the ultimate destination of the transfer road, but expect society soon to take another road. With their disposition to expect the best possible outcome, optimists dwell on the most hopeful aspects of the situation. Trust men, they assure us, and they will be true in the end; expect greatness and they will show themselves great. Trust America, it will remain the home of freedom and the hope of the world.

Changes in human affairs are the work of changes in moral standards. The American transfer system with all its political power is an elaborate product of contemporary standards. It is changing continually as the public perception of right conduct is changing, which wields more power than the U.S. Congress and a thousand judges. Changes are cosmopolitan, sweeping across national boundaries, affecting human affairs everywhere. Governments cannot prevent them; they may smother them and coercion may suppress them temporarily, but nothing can prevent them for long.

American economic conditions may deteriorate because false ideas may guide the body politic towards stagnation and disintegration; but conditions elsewhere may improve rapidly because economic policies are guided by inexorable economic law. They may deteriorate slowly in the U.S. and improve visibly in Japan, Hong Kong or Singapore. They may deteriorate in Mexico, but improve in Argentina, always in direct proportion to man's moral order. When economic conditions are improving elsewhere while they are deteriorating in the U.S., the American people may repent of their ways and return to the proven road. The success of more prosperous societies may set the example.

The American people may remember someday that, in order to sustain human life and well-being, they must labor. Income and wealth are the fruits of individual effort and service; to extract them from each other by political force is both immoral and counterproductive. Political largesse raises an army of idle beneficiaries, promotes consumption without production and discourages effort and thrift. Transfer income by political force is worse than no income at all. The transfer state openly and officially hampers economic output. It may erect production barriers, impose tariffs and quotas, parity prices and acreage restrictions; it may resort to inflation, credit expansion, and deficit spending. It tends to be self-destructive.

An American Freedom Party may some day put an end to political intervention designed to favor half the population at the expense of the other half and to reduce the supply of goods and render them more expensive. An organization of persons united for the purpose of influencing government policy toward greater economic well-being may signal the end of the transfer system. Although recent history contains many sordid and selfish chapters, political parties may be powerful forces for good in a free society. A Freedom Party may educate and organize public opinion by keeping the people informed on the follies of policies restricting output, reducing supplies and benefiting some voters at the expense of others. It may contribute to civic education, present candidates for public offices, and serve to represent millions of Americans who are interested in rising standards of living and lower goods prices.

Many American voters are women who are homemakers and mothers. It is difficult to believe that, if they were informed, they would cast their votes for benefits and bounty for themselves and debts for their children. American women are the natural members of a Freedom Party that opposes policies designed to restrict production, to raise prices, and to favor one social class at the expense of another. Young people who are vitally interested in the preservation of the apparatus of production are their natural allies. The present system has made youth the primary beast of burden and victim of transfer; the most monstrous burden, Social Security and Medicare, has been placed squarely on the shoulders of youth. An American Freedom Party would show mercy and promptly remove the horrid load.

No affliction nor temptation should induce us to despair. It is necessary to hope, for hope itself is happiness and the beginning of reform.

Dr. Sennholz is chairman of the department of economics at Grove City College in Pennsylvania, and a former chairman of the Board of Trustees at FEE. He is a well-known writer and lecturer on economic, political, and monetary affairs.

---

1. Hans F. Sennholz, *Debts and Deficits* (Spring Mills, Pa.: Libertarian Press), pp. 32–42.

2. Peter J. Ferrara explores important philosophical questions in his *Social Security* (Washington, D.C.: Cato Institute, 1980); he also edited *Social Security, Prospects for Real*

Reform, which is an up-to-date analysis of the continuing problems of the System (Washington, D.C.: Cato Institute, 1985); cf. also Douglas Brown, *An American Philosophy of Social Security* (Princeton, N.J.: Princeton University Press, 1972); Edwin E. Witte, the *Development of the Social Security Act* (Madison, Wisc.: The University of Wisconsin Press, 1972); Joseph A. Pechman, Henry J. Aaron, and Michael K. Taussig, *Social Security: Perspectives for Reform* (Washington, D.C.: Brookings Institution, 1968); Alicia H. Munnell, *The Future of Social Security* (Washington, D.C.: Brookings Institution, 1977).

3. Cf. Hans F. Sennholz, *Social Security, Is Reform Possible?* (Grove City, Pa.: Public Policy Education Fund, Inc., 1981).

4. Hans F. Sennholz, "Another Federal Catastrophe" *Private Practice* (Shawnee, Okla.: CCMS Publishing Co.), Vol. 18, No. 4, April 1986, p. 21 *et seq*; John C. Goodman, *The Regulation of Medical Care: Is the Price Too High?* (Washington, D.C.: Cato Institute, 1980).

5. *Congressional Quarterly, Almanac,* 99th Congress, 2nd Session, 1986 (Washington, D.C.: Congressional Quarterly Inc.), pp. 258, 261; cf. also Cheryl Russell on the fear of AIDS ending the sexual revolution, *The Wall Street Journal,* 3/30/1987, p. 18; Gary North, "The Plague Has Come at Last," *Remnant Review,* Vol 14, No. 5, March 6, 1987 (Fort Worth, Texas: Remnant Review).

6. *Facts on File,* March 8, 1985 (New York: Facts on File, Inc.), p. 151.

7. *Budget of the U.S. Government,* Fiscal Year 1987, pp. 4-15.

The Primacy of Freedom

BY BRIAN SUMMERS

THERE is a time to ask basic questions. Now, as we mark the retirement of Dr. Paul L. Poirot, who has contributed so much time, energy, and wisdom to the cause of liberty, it is perhaps appropriate for each of us to ask himself: Why should I follow this man's lead and dedicate myself to advancing the freedom philosophy?

On the surface, this seems like a trivial question. Liberty is good, and we should devote ourselves to good causes. But, as we all know, there are other things we can do with our lives and other ways to spend our money. Why is liberty so important that we should devote our efforts toward it when there are so many other worthy causes which cry for our attention and support?

One way to answer is to point out that the freedom philosophy, according to all available evidence, is correct. Both rational thought and historical study demonstrate that the free market, private property, limited government system works—it delivers higher living standards than any alternate system. If truth be known, then it is our duty to advance it.

But the same applies to other disciplines. We can find truth in mathematics, the arts, the sciences, and at least parts of various philosophical systems. If one's concern is the truth—and I believe that our allegiance to the truth must precede our commitment to any endeavor—then the freedom philosophy should have no greater claim on our lives than any other demonstrably true system.

But the freedom philosophy is concerned with more than the truth. It is concerned with people. It analyzes the institutions and laws which enable people to prosper and grow, as well as the institutions and laws which have brought destitution, suffering, and death to millions of victims. The freedom philosophy is important because people are important.

This is not to trivialize other disciplines or to say that no one should work in a field which, for some of us, is less important than our overriding concern with freedom. If everyone were working for liberty to the exclusion of everything else, there would be no farmers, craftsmen, doctors, or any of the other people who keep us alive. Furthermore, if all intellectuals concerned themselves exclusively with the freedom philosophy, the world might be a freer place, but it would be devoid of the arts which enrich so many lives.

However, I think that, from time to time, we should take a long-term look at things. Sure, the arts and sciences are important. What would life be without them? But I think we also should give some thought to the institutions which enable such disciplines to flourish. We should ask ourselves why so many human advances have come from relatively free societies. We should ask why totalitarian nations not only have to steal our technology, they can't even feed their own people.

Consider, in particular, medical care. I marvel at the advances in medicine and medical technology, and I applaud those who freely contribute their time and wealth to support medical care and research. There is no belittling their contribution. But again, I think it is important to give some thought to the social system which creates the wealth we contribute, as well as consider the institutions which best facilitate an adequate diet, sanitation, techno-logical, biological, and chemical advances, and which foster a spirit of open inquiry. It also is instructive to consider first-hand reports of people who have witnessed the appalling medical systems in totalitarian states.

If, as I contend, the freedom philosophy is so important, the question then becomes—not why should anyone devote his life to advancing this philos-ophy—but why don't *more* people work for liberty? Why—when resources are being squandered at an incredible rate, when billions of people continue to suffer in abject poverty, when statism unleashes its fury in seemingly endless wars and acts of terrorism—why doesn't the great mass of humanity cry "Enough!" and throw off the shackles of enslaving governments?

A Lack of Understanding

The answer, in short, is that they don't understand. And we shouldn't be surprised, since in most cases, people never have been told the basic precepts of the freedom philosophy. For more than a generation, the task of explaining these precepts has fallen largely on the shoulders of Paul Poirot, his colleagues at The Foundation for Economic Education, and the authors and speakers who work with this Foundation.

It is difficult to measure the success of these educational efforts. However, we see encouraging signs in our daily contacts with friends and acquain-tances, as well as in the mass media. In particular, there seems to be a growing awareness of the need for economic incentives, of the dangers of protectionism, and of the disruptive consequences of an expansionary monetary policy.

This is a start. And FEE has played a major role in this growing understanding of basic economics. In fact, it can be argued that The Foundation for Economic Education has been the wellspring of this understanding. One can make an impressive list of the educators, journalists, clergymen, and political leaders who have received our publications and attended our seminars.

But this is not enough. For one thing, the level of economic illiteracy is still appalling. How many people can explain the causes of the Great Depression? How many know that the gas lines which plagued us in the 1970s had nothing to do with OPEC, and everything to do with price controls? How many have any understanding of how government spending is diverting billions of dollars from our nation's capital base? The list could be expanded almost at will.

Beyond the baneful consequences of economic illiteracy lies an even more troubling failing—the inability to make connections. The next time there is a documentary about war, or famine, or death camps, watch it. Look long and hard at the suffering faces. Then ask yourself why these things happen. Can you explain why these are not natural occurrences, that they have economic and philosophical causes?

Or visit a hospital and marvel at the medicines and medical technology. Can you explain why these advances are available now, after several centuries of relative freedom in a few capitalist countries, while for thousands of years and in most nations the diseases we now conquer as a matter of course were a death sentence? Why here? Why now? And why not sooner?

I will not attempt to answer these and similar questions in the space of this essay. These questions have been raised and answered for more than a generation in the pages of *The Freeman*, FEE's various books and pamphlets, and FEE lectures and seminars. The Foundation for Economic Education asks the important questions, and hundreds of thousands of lives have been influenced by this Foundation's work.

But even if we could reach every man, woman, and child with sound economic arguments, even if we could sit them all down and lecture to them on economics for a month, it still wouldn't be enough, because economics isn't enough. Economics isn't even the most important part of the case for freedom. This, in fact, is the primary thing for those of us engaged in economic education to remember.

The only reason I can down-play the role of economics in advancing the cause of liberty is that there is something which is so much more important: moral principles. Freedom is right because it is morally right. Government intervention in peaceful affairs—no matter at whose behest, and no matter what the excuse—is wrong.

Fortunately, while many people are turned off by economic arguments or have trouble with abstract concepts, almost everyone has some understanding of right and wrong. The difficulty is in getting them to see that the free market, private property, limited government system is the only social system in keeping with sound moral principles. There is further difficulty in convincing people that when government, acting as someone's agent, harms one person to benefit another, then the person who used the government for his own ends is as guilty of plundering another as if he had committed the act himself.

But this moral education can be done. In fact, for more than thirty years, Paul Poirot and his various authors did a masterful job of explaining moral principles and showing how they apply to public issues as well as to private matters.

By and large, *The Freeman* has been the only publication doing this vitally important work of attracting people to the freedom philosophy by presenting the free market, private property, limited government system as an ideal moral system—one we would want our children to inherit. This, more than anything else, is what has made The Foundation for Economic Education not only unique, but what makes it the hub of the entire freedom movement.

Let us thus, at this occasion, thank Paul Poirot for his tireless efforts, his wise counsel, and his steadfast commitment to the highest principles—and rededicate ourselves to upholding the moral principles which are the key to our success as individuals, as a Foundation, and as a nation.

Mr. Summers is senior editor of The Freeman.

The Transformation of "Liberalism"

BY JOHN K. WILLIAMS

ONLY a person consumed by self-hatred would ascribe to himself or herself the adjective "illiberal." The term itself derives from the Latin *illiberalis,* meaning "mean" or "sordid." The word is defined in *The Oxford English Dictionary* by such expressions as "not befitting or of the nature of a free man," "not generous in respect to the opinions, rights, or liberty of others," "narrow-minded, bigoted," and "base, mean, vulgar, rude, sordid."

Paul Poirot is the antithesis of the "illiberal" person. A graciousness and a generosity inform his professional activities and personal relationships. He never confuses breadth of spirit with shallowness of insight, never lets a warm tolerance degenerate into a superficial indifference, never identifies an open mind with an empty head. As one of the many people unspeakably enriched by him—both through the pages of *The Freeman* and as a colleague—I am proud to have been asked to honor in this volume a man in whom the principles of the freedom philosophy have found a compelling incarnation.

Yet the irony is that Paul Poirot has been denied, by the debasement of language, a label—"liberal"—which, if one is interested to track back words to their original signification, superbly describes him. Men and women violently opposed to the ideas and ideals which, expounded by thinkers such as John Locke, David Hume, Adam Smith, and Thomas Jefferson, once constituted "liberalism" have somehow managed to capture and press into their service a word, and claim for themselves the honorable pedigree still attached to that word.

The anything but flattering connotations of the word "illiberal" may, perhaps, explain why it is that men and women committed to ideas and ideals anathema to the constitutive principles of "liberalism" as originally understood—private property rights, government limited to the task of protecting the equal human rights of all citizens, and an essentially unfettered market economy—have tenaciously clung to the word "liberalism" whilst transforming its original signification. Yet whatever the "why" of the transformation, that transformation most certainly has been effected.

Liberty, Government and Rights

Liberalism in its classical mode defined the role of government very simply. Its task was to protect the individual from actual or threatened violence, theft or fraud. Government existed to secure and protect individual freedom, and freedom signified simply "freedom *from* human-created constraints," constraints typically finding expression in laws which proscribed for some activities permitted to others.

Frequently linked with this understanding both of the role of government and of the nature of liberty was a *negative* doctrine of human rights. Essentially, this doctrine affirmed *that a "right" of A to do X or to own Y signified the absence of an obligation to refrain from doing X or to surrender Y.* This "right" of A implied a correlative obligation for people other than A—the obligation *not* to force A to refrain from doing X or to surrender Y.

The English philosopher Thomas Hill Green (1836–1882) directly challenged this understanding of the role of government and of the nature of liberty, and indirectly challenged this negative understanding of "rights." Liberty signifies, insisted Green, not simply an absence of humanly imposed constraints but the actual possession of a "positive power" or "capacity" to engage in some activity. Government's task is not simply that of protecting an individual from coercive restraints imposed by other human beings, but of positively fostering an individual's power or capacity effectively to engage in an activity. "Freedom" signifies not simply "freedom *from* external constraint" but "freedom successfully *to* engage in an activity." Simply, a person is "free" to climb a mountain if and only if that person (1) is not obligated to refrain from attempting to climb it, and (2) possesses the capacity, and perhaps the equipment, necessary successfully to climb it!

Thus was the way paved from a *negative* analysis of the word "right" to a *positive* analysis. Alan Gewirth, an extraordinarily sophisticated moral and political philosopher, perhaps most eloquently today defends this analysis (*Reason and Morality* [Chicago: University of Chicago Press, 1978]). An individual, A, he argues, has, simply by virtue of his or her capacity to engage in purposeful activity, a "right" to freedom (crudely, noninterference by others) *and* a "right" to well-being. Correlative to these "rights" of A are obligations of people other than A *both* not coercively to interfere with A's peaceful autonomous behavior *and* to provide A with the goods and services necessary for his or her "well-being."

Thomas Hill Green did not perceive himself as drastically changing the classical liberals' analysis of the role of government, of liberty, or of "rights." He categorically rejected the statism of Hegel, insisting that "we cannot significantly speak of freedom except with reference to individual persons" (*Lectures on the Principles of Political Obligation* [Ann Arbor: University of Michigan Press, 1967] p. 8). Indeed, the transition from what one might call a "protective" model of government to a "providing" model of government had been facilitated by John Stuart Mill. In *On Liberty* Mill had failed dismally to reconcile his enthusiasm for the principles of *laissez faire* and his sympathy for the practices of socialism. He *de facto* threw his lot in with the latter when he allowed that "a state ought to be considered as a great benefit society, or mutual insurance company, for helping (under the necessary regulations for preventing abuse) that large proportion of its members who cannot help themselves." Even had Mill elaborated and justified "the necessary regulations for preventing abuse," the crucial move leading to the transformation of the classical liberals' understanding of government had been effected.

Yet an even more significant contribution to the transformation of the nature of liberalism must be "credited" to Mill. The welfarist function of the state, crucial to contemporary "liberalism," rests in part upon an essentially economic distinction, a distinction clearly made by Mill but rarely discussed.

Production and Distribution

In his justly famous *Principles of Political Economy* Mill pens these words: "The laws and conditions of the production of wealth, partake of the character of physical truths. There is nothing optional or arbitrary in them. . . . [T]his is not so with the distribution of wealth. The things once there, mankind, individually or collectively, can do with them as they like." (7th edition, p. 200)

The primary distinction here made by Mill is between the productive capacity of the free market in a free society and the distribution of goods and services effected by such a politico-economic system. That distinction has today become all but ubiquitous.

- Many "compromising" defenders of a partially-free market economy simultaneously laud the productive genius of the market and lament the alleged "inequities" characterizing the distribution an unfettered market economy would effect. "Naturally, I am not defending *laissez-faire* capitalism with all its injustices. We must, minimally, 'redistribute' in a fair and equitable way what the market produces. . . . "
- An increasing number of self-styled socialists are rejecting the old-style model of centralized, socialist planning. At a theoretical level, works such as Peter Rutland's *The Myth of the Plan* come to mind. At what one might call the "practical" level one cannot but be aware of the belated rediscovery of markets in many Eastern European nations, the nervous flirtation with markets in Communist China and Gorbachev's Russia,

and the extraordinary enthusiasm for markets voiced by "democratic" socialists in numerous Western nations, including my native Australia. Yet the claim is repeatedly made that reliance upon the market for wealth production in no way entails a reliance upon the market's distribution of wealth. A distribution of goods and services informed by the essentially egalitarian vision of socialism must be effected.

Simply, the contemporary "liberal" vision has been modified by grim economic reality. The free market is requisite if the goods and services sufficient for all more or less equally to enjoy a "good life," materially defined, are to be produced. Yet since the market's productivity is allegedly distinct from the profoundly unequal holdings of goods and services effected by the market, the latter can be corrected and made to conform to the egalitarianism informing the "liberal" model of a "just social order." The productivity of the market, plus the pattern of wealth allocation dictated by "distributive justice," brings, if not Utopia, at least the "good society," within the power of human beings to realize.

Yet *can* one distinguish, as does Mill, between production and distribution in a free market economy? I think not.

To what must the productive genius of a free market economy be ascribed? The voluntary exchanging of goods and services? Surely not: Such exchanges have taken place from the very beginnings of human history on this planet. Jerusalem of early biblical days was a market city—a place where people exchanged the products of their labors—as were all the great cities of the ancient world.

Oddly, two French historians once hailed by the "Left" have reminded a forgetful world of what sound but all too widely ignored economists long had realized. Jean Baechler, in his scintillating work *The Origins of Capitalism* (trans B. Cooper [Oxford: Basil Blackwell, 1975]) and Fernand Braudel, in his magisterial three-volume study *Civilization and Capitalism: 15th–18th Century* (trans S. Reynolds [New York: Harper and Row, 1984]) have documented in painstaking detail the appearance, in sixteenth-century England and the Netherlands, of an unprecedented phenomenon: sustained economic growth. Human beings stumbled their accidental way into, or in a few cases actually reasoned out, changed practices which increased the productivity of their labors. So far, so familiar. The goods and services available to a community increased. Again, so far so familiar. The mortality rate decreased and life expectancy increased. Nothing new about that. But the old Malthusian trap that, for millennia, had cursed humankind was somehow foiled! The rate at which productivity increased surpassed the rate at which population increased. Every new birth was hailed as a potential source of creativity rather than cursed as yet another mouth to be fed. The grim joke played by a seemingly cruel cosmos had come to an end.

Why did this unprecedented phenomenon—sustained economic growth—appear when it did and where it did? The old answers fail to work. No new technologies or empires or elsewhere unavailable supplies of raw materials can be posited. One and only one reality makes sense of what in truth happened. In sixteenth-century England and the Netherlands a new system of property rights was conceived. In its embryonic form, the system of universal private property later defended by Adam Smith and his fellow classical liberals had been conceived. The rudimentary beginnings of the free market economy in a free society had appeared upon the earth, and the age-old specters of famine and destitution began to fade away.

From whence this new system of property rights? The story is complex, but in large part the system derived from ideas about human nature which were rediscovered during the Protestant Reformation and the Catholic counter-Reformation. What is significant is that changing ideas led to changing legal and political structures, and that these in turn led to a drastic change in humanity's economic lot.

What, one might well ask, has the above historical aside to do with Mill's distinction between the productive capacity of a market economy and the distribution of goods and services effected by such an economy? Let me make explicit my argument: *A market economy depends upon a system of private property rights.*

Given such a system, there is at no stage of the productive process a stock of "unowned goods"—machinery is owned, money to pay workers in the present for goods to be sold in the future, if ever, is owned, incompletely produced goods are owned, completed goods are owned. It is precisely because this is the case, that the market so efficiently allocates resources and so bountifully generates wealth.

A politically determined distribution of the goods and services produced by the market thus demands a prior expropriation of these goods from their "rightful" owners.

Such a distribution therefore interferes with and drastically modifies the process whereby the goods are created.

Simply, if Mill is correct in insisting that the laws of economics—the processes whereby wealth is created—are not "optional or arbitrary," and if private property rights, precisely defined and efficiently enforced are crucial rather than incidental to these processes, the alleged distinction between the production of wealth and the distribution of wealth collapses.

And with it collapses a crucial tenet of many contemporary "liberals."

Epilogue

Those of us espousing the freedom philosophy so cogently defended by Paul Poirot can with justice resent the "linguistic imperialism" displayed by the collectivists' capture of the word "liberal." Yet in the last analysis what matters are the realities words signify, not the words themselves. One would be surprised to learn that Paul Poirot was in any way agitated by his being denied a word to describe himself and his philosophy. His concern was to recover not a word but liberty and the realities that make for liberty. May that concern be ours.

The Reverend Dr. John K. Williams has been a teacher and is a free-lance writer and lecturer in North Melbourne, Victoria, Australia. He has been resident scholar at FEE for the past three summers.

The Unnoticed Erosion of the Meaning and Value of Liberty

BY ANNE WORTHAM

IN AN ARTICLE on the failure of socialism in the case of subsidized cotton production, Paul Poirot lists the following circumstances that, according to socialist theory, are ideal for an experiment in socialism: a well-developed industrial society; a wealthy people who have known the productivity and abundance of private capitalism and who could afford such costs as a socialistic experiment might involve; a complex exchange economy with many highly skilled and highly productive specialists from whom goods and services might be drawn; persons who would submit willingly to identification and classification as deserving dependents of the society. "Such an experiment surely would be facilitated," he writes, "if all the people had been more or less conditioned for controls—perhaps having experienced a series of world wars, much international bickering and unrest, a prolonged period of heavy taxation, a huge government debt—yes, and a debauched currency."[1]

On these criteria, says Poirot, no country has been a better testing ground for socialism than the United States during the years since the depth of The Great Depression. "When and where else in the world has there been more skilled planning, more effective control, more able and willing participation, and less resistance and interference? We've been taught socialism in the schools, read it in the papers, heard it on the radio, seen it on television, and even lived it in our daily affairs." Surely, he observes, interest groups like cotton growers "have been well-organized and persistent in acknowledging and proclaiming their need. And who on earth has stood and denied it?"[2]

Another question one might ask is why those who do protest the experiment are denigrated as enemies of liberty? Leonard Read has answered this question in the following observation: "Most Americans are unaware of a decline in individual liberty, and the reason is obvious: the decline rarely takes the form of sudden personal deprivations but, instead, takes the form of unnoticed erosion, and thus, we come, as do the Russians, to regard whatever state we are in as a normal condition."[3]

Since liberty has lost its importance, wrote Read, people are not aware that it is in jeopardy. They cannot recognize that the American socialist revolution "is no longer an event of the future to be feared; it is a catastrophe of the past to be remedied—and remembered. In short, the revolution *was*, that is, the socialist objective has been achieved. Few people seem to appreciate the terrible fact that, already, we are subject to a centralized government of unlimited power."[4]

How has this state of affairs come to be? How is it that people who proclaim every 4th of July that theirs is the land of the free—how could these same people be so ignorant of the decline of their freedom? There are many explanations. My answer is that it could not have happened if the American passion for equality had not superseded the imperatives of liberty to the point of rendering them "impractical" in the minds of many people, and if egalitarians had not succeeded in using ideas of liberty to justify statist goals.

Equality is no longer used in reference to man's nature as a reasoning and self-determining being; it is now the means by which individuals redefine their nature and their relationship to other men and to political authority. It no longer refers to equal political freedom, but is understood by most Americans to mean equality of condition or equality of result. It has acquired such moral and political legitimacy that even in the face of national debt, declining industrial power, and the further erosion of civil liberties, Americans continue to demand it without realizing how much they are sacrificing for a goal that is impossible to achieve. Why do Americans willingly sacrifice their freedom for an ideal that cannot be realized? How did the goal of equality of condition attain such plausibility?

Equality of condition has triumphed over freedom by making itself the end to which freedom is the means. And this has been accomplished by redefining ideas of liberty, transforming them into self-nullifying "anti-concepts"[5] that eliminate the difference between freedom and servility and obscure the oppressive effects of equalitarian policies. In order to diminish the meaning of ideas of liberty, egalitarians equate the conception of freedom as absence of constraint with freedom as collective self-determination; they redefine rights to mean "needs," "interests," or "privileges;" they set up false dichotomies between inequality and equity, between equality and merit, between people and property. In the face of the philosophical chaos that remains, it is not surprising that many Americans conceive of freedom as (to quote a line from a popular song of the Sixties) "just another word for nothing else to lose." The arbitrary manipulation of meanings has been so successful that many Americans are hopelessly incapable of recognizing liberty's eclipse by equality. (And there are many who recognize it with approval.)

A review of the use to which some of the key ideas of liberty are being put will further illuminate the extent of the ideological attack on the legitimacy of individual liberty. This discussion will focus on equality, individual rights, equal opportunity, and equity.

Equality and inequality are two sides of the same coin: human nature. As a species, mankind is universally characterized and distinguished from other species by the capacity to reason. It is with respect to this aspect of human identity that all individuals included in the species are equal. The species is also characterized by a high degree of variety, diversity, and differentiation—that is, inequality—rooted both in the biological and cultural nature of man. Thus, all people are equal in human nature, but not uniform in human attributes. *Regardless* of biological and cultural heritage, social status, economic position, competence, character and achievement, every person can say, "I am human." And every person, *because* of these same attributes, can say: "I am I, unlike any other human before or after me." Inequality is itself an attribute of the human species. To achieve the equalitarian ideal of a uniform species, or uniform group attributes, would require transcending the very order of nature itself, which in turn would entail violating the nature of man. Therefore, it should be dismissed as a goal. For, in reality, there is no conflict between natural equality of the human species and the social inequality resulting from man's individuation and differentiation.

In a mixed economy the ideal of equality of result is offered as an alternative to all inequality, whether just or unjust. It is an absurd notion that cannot work in practice. It can only be pursued at the expense of liberty and result in the further institutionalization of unjust inequality. But its proponents boldly argue that today's sacrifice of liberty to equality is the only way of achieving liberty at some undetermined time in the future. The ultimate goal of these egalitarians is to negate the principle of individual rights and to legitimate the idea that some men have the right to violate the rights of others.

Why is the negation of individual rights so important to egalitarians? Rights are those conditions of existence that are required for man's proper survival and moral principles that define the extent of man's freedom of action in a social context.[6] The fundamental nature of rights is that they are exclusive to the individual, not the family, the group, the society, or the nation. They are not permissions, privileges, or conditions granted to men by social institutions, by the law, or by one's neighbors. Individual rights are not arbitrary constructs created by man, but absolute requirements of man's nature. It is not in the interest of egalitarians that men hold this conception of rights, for such men will not permit themselves to be ruled by another. In a free society, rights are seen as necessary conditions of individual liberty. In a mixed economy freedom is seen as a characteristic of the social whole, and rights are correspondingly defined as pertaining not to the individual, but to the collective—from the species ("human" rights) to interest groups ("women's/gay/black/family/patients'/ farmers' " rights).

It is only the principle of individual rights that gives meaning to the concept of equality in the social context. As an abstract measurement of man's political relationship to other men and to political authority, equality means that (1) all men have equal status before the law; and (2) each person should enjoy equal conditions of civil freedom and equal protection of his freedom in order that he may achieve whatever goals his own intelligence, ability, and productivity will allow.

Just as the principle of individual rights gives meaning to political equality, so does it give meaning to the concept of "opportunity." Opportunities are conditions of human existence that are favorable for the attainment of a goal. They are not self-evident requirements of man's nature, as rights are, but must be discovered by his mind and brought into existence by his effort. (Even opportunities that we retrospectively identify as "strokes of luck" would be lost opportunities without the effort that gave them substance.) They are not unlimited, as those of one man end where the rights of another begin. In a free society equal opportunity would not be taken to mean that everybody ought to begin at the same starting place. Rather, the ethical-political content of equal opportunity is that since man's survival depends on self-sustaining and self-generated action, he must be free from interference to peacefully take this action in pursuit of the resources on which his life depends. It is on the basis of the principle of equal opportunity—the equal political freedom to choose one's actions independently—that toleration and limited government are defended.

In a mixed economy the idea of equal opportunity is used to justify the restriction of the pursuits of men whose social position and productivity places them at an advantage over men of lesser ability. It is used to redefine equal freedom to *pursue* life chances to mean equal *consequences* of the pursuit. John Gray summarized the "positive" view of freedom underlying this contemporary liberal conception of equal opportunity as follows:

> it is the view that individual freedom in the full sense involves having an opportunity for self-realization . . . The political content of the positive view is that, if certain resources, powers or abilities are needed for self-realization to be effectively achievable, then having these resources must be considered part of freedom itself. It is on this basis that modern revisionary liberals have defended the welfare state as a freedom-enhancing institution: it is alleged to confer needed resources on individuals and thereby to expand their chances of freedom. These revisionary liberals [hold the view] that liberty (positive liberty) involves more than having the legal right to act. It signifies, primarily and centrally, having the resources and opportunities to act so as to make the best of one's life.[7]

Equity is another idea of liberty that is used to undermine the legitimacy of individual freedom. As Aristotle wrote, equity is "genuine justice," based on man's rational nature. The exercise of justice is the recognition that every person must be judged for what he is. In a free society equity would involve the practice of judging a person's character and actions exclusively on the basis of the factual evidence available, and of evaluating them by means of an objective moral criterion. Individuals are judged as *individuals*, not as bearers of the attributes of social categories such as race, sex, and age; neither are they judged as representatives of groups with which they may be affiliated or of "statistical populations." In a mixed economy equity is used to obliterate the concept of justice and substitute it with the idea of "social justice"— the practice of redistributing income, status and political authority on the basis of collective rights. Equity is employed to suggest that there is no difference between the group and the individual, between a person's physical attributes and his character; it disregards the difference between the earned or deserved and the unearned or undeserved, between men's virtues and their vices, between innocence and guilt, between rational self-interest and self-sacrifice. It gives plausibility to paying men for material goods they have not produced, rewarding them for achievements they have not attained, penalizing them for achievements that are theirs; it enables men to sever the connection between the qualities of a person's character and the admiration and respect extended to or denied him. It is no wonder that in such a society, the prevailing attitude is that life is unfair and justice unattainable.

The undermining of the meaning and importance of liberty, and its diminishment in practical life began before the creation of the Republic. One of the significant early blows to liberty came during the nation's revolutionary birth when some members of the Continental Congress insisted that Thomas Jefferson delete from the draft of the Declaration of Independence the passage in which he charged King George III of England with violating the "most sacred rights of life and liberty" of the Negroes who were sold into slavery. While the American revolutionaries declared to the world their independence of a distant monarchy, they neglected to pursue the freedom of bondsmen who found themselves in the New World through no choice of their own.

Are Men Naturally Free?

The creation of history's first country of individual liberty and the establishment of a political system which stressed the right of each man to the preservation of his own life, the ownership of the fruits of his labor, and the pursuit of his own happiness was the American answer to key questions posed by the Age of Enlightenment: Are men naturally free? If all are free, should they enjoy equal political freedom? This was the issue to which the Declaration of Independence spoke. It was the issue over which the question of slavery was eventually argued. It stirred advocates of women's suffrage, and moved blacks and whites who protested government-enforced racial segregation and discrimination. And it is the issue yet to be faced in deciding the unresolved fate of American Indians.

The issue of whether a man is the owner of his person and life or the "property" of another human being was settled by the Thirteenth Amendment of the United States Constitution. The Fourteenth, Fifteenth, and Nineteenth Amendments asserted every person's equal right to freedom and established laws to protect that right. Theoretically, the issue of political equality was resolved and Americans, regardless of sex, race, creed or national origin, could get on with the business of realizing a free and independent existence for themselves.

But the guarantee of political equality has not been sufficient for many Americans. As they see it, the guarantees of equal political freedom and equal protection under the law lack sufficient power to unite so complex a society. A "more perfect union" can only be realized if Americans are united by the establishment of group rights and equality of condition. Americans of this modern liberal persuasion view freedom as a *means*, as opposed to classical liberalism's conception of freedom as an *end*.[8] Thus, they believe the aim of equality of condition by means of collective rights should be sought, even if it requires assigning greater political authority to the state than is provided by the Constitution. Indeed, many propose that the Constitution be amended to require the state to carry out these goals.

The sentiment underlying the advocacy of government-imposed social and economic equality has been present in American society since before the amendment of the Bill of Rights to the Constitution. When Alexis de Tocqueville visited America in the 1830s he observed the boisterous egalitarianism of Jacksonian democracy and concluded that perhaps greater than their passion for freedom was the Americans' search for "complete equality." Their passion for equality was "ardent, insatiable, incessant, invincible; they call for equality in freedom; and if they cannot obtain that they still call for equality in slavery." Democracy, he observed, was viewed as "the means for everyone to rise to the level of everyone else."[9]

During the two generations between the Civil War and the First World War when American society was being transformed by industrialization and urbanization, the American passion for freedom was overtaken by the passion for equality. The "old" individualism of the American Enlightenment—the philosophy of natural freedom—was rejected and by the beginning of the twentieth century, Americans were being introduced to a new set of ideas to justify their clamor for equality. John Dewey was one of the leading formulators of those ideas, which became known as American pragmatism.

Dewey wrote that Americans must "get away from the conception of the individual as an isolated and independent unit;" they must turn their backs on the "rigid doctrine of natural rights inherent in individuals independent of social organization."[10] The "peculiar idea of personal liberty" must be discarded; the "artificial" autonomy attributed to the individual by Enlightenment thinkers must be rejected for a view of the individual as a "socialized" participant in the social process.[11] In viewing the motives of the individual, we should place less emphasis on "calculating self-interest" and regard them more in terms of social responsibility.[12] As for the standards by which men are to approach social problems, Dewey argued that we cannot cure social ills with "magnificent generalizations" like freedom and order, individualism and socialism, culture and unity, actuality and tradition, etc. We can resolve social antagonisms only with the trial and error of the experimental method.[13] Since thought constructs the objects of knowledge, and since all knowledge is practical, man may "construct" in his mind any social environment he deems practical for "the all-around growth of every member of society."[14] And the test of what is practical is that which proves instrumental.

John Dewey provided just the philosophy that muckrakers and populists in the Progressive movement needed.[15] If he was the "guru" of the movement, Theodore Roosevelt, the first president of the twentieth century, was its publicity man.[16] Roosevelt's doctrine, which was alternately called a "Square Deal" and the "new nationalism," held that "social justice" could be attained only through strengthening the power of the federal government so that the executive could be the "steward of public welfare." The judiciary must not disrupt this stewardship; contrary to its traditional position, it must "be interested primarily in human welfare rather than property." Indeed, this must be the position of the American nation. Men thinking primarily of property rights and personal profits "must now give way to the advocate of human welfare, who rightly maintains that every man hold his property subject to the general right of the community to regulate its use to whatever degree the public welfare may require it."[17]

This doctrine influenced not only the two presidents immediately following Roosevelt, but also every president from Franklin Roosevelt to Ronald Reagan. The cumulative effect of their varying implementation of this policy of statism is that America is now a society in which the quest for political equality has been abandoned for the quest for equality of condition. Individual rights have been sacrificed to group rights. The "public good" has replaced individual self-interest. The tyranny of "affirmative action" has usurped the standards of excellence and merit. Individual initiative has become ensnared in the trap of "social responsibility." The noble ideal of individual liberty has been transformed into a revolt against the very self-responsibility and risk-taking that liberty entails. And the politics of victimization is the order of the day.[18]

In a society based on individual rights, political freedom, and capitalism, there is no conflict between inequality, equity, and merit. Inequality resulting from people's varying application of their abilities to the problems of living is not synonymous with systemic injustice, unfairness, or institutional discrimination. One man's gain is not another's loss; one social class or group does not improve its life chances at the expense of the life chances of other classes or groups.[19] No one is exempt from the risks and responsibilities of exchange and competition in the open, unregulated market of goods, services, and ideas. The consequence of this expression of freedom is the unequal but wide-ranging and equitable distribution of knowledge, wealth, consumption, and authority.

In a free society laws and institutions reflect people's recognition of the fact that it is neither just nor unjust that men are born with differing natural abilities into different social positions. Therefore those possessing great natural capacity and who are at a more favorable starting point in society are not made to atone for what is not an injustice and not of their making. Neither are there attempts to eliminate these differences, or put them to work for the greatest number, or for the worst off. In a free society laws and judicial and political institutions are limited to ensuring that such differences among citizens are allowed free expression that does not infringe on the rights of others.

The American society is no longer organized primarily according to private capitalism; rather, it is organized according to the mixture of freedom and controls of welfare state capitalism. In this system private groups (e.g., labor, education, business) that have governmental power without governmental responsibility compete for exemption from open competition.[20] In this system there exists the concurrence of just inequality on the one hand and unjust exploitative inequality on the other.[21] Social mobility in America is dictated by a system of legalized constraints that benefit some at the expense of others.

This zero-sum system of privileges and penalties prevails not because it is either the best ethical or practical arrangement. Rather, it exists because, at bottom, most Americans believe that security and certainty are corollaries of freedom, that they have a right to these conditions of life, and that it is the duty of the government to provide them. This belief—that freedom requires state paternalism—reflects a profound ignorance of the theoretical and practical meaning of freedom. But it is the prevailing idea of the American political culture.

Dr. Wortham is a visiting scholar at the Hoover Institution in Stanford, California.

---

1. Paul Poirot, "Socialism at Its Best," *Essays on Liberty*, Vol. V (September 1958), The Foundation for Economic Education.

2. *Ibid.*

3. Leonard E. Read, *How to Advance Liberty* (Irvington-on-Hudson, NY: The Foundation for Economic Education, 1965).

4. *Ibid.*

5. Ayn Rand identifies "anti-concept" as an "artificial, unnecessary, and (rationally) unusable term, designed to replace and obliterate some legitimate concepts . . . without public discussion; and, as a means to that end, to make public discussion unintelligible, and to induce the same disintegration in the mind of any man who accepts them, rendering him incapable of clear thinking or rational judgment." See: Ayn Rand, *Capitalism: the Unknown Ideal* (New York: The New American Library, 1966), pp. 176–177.

6. *Ibid.*, pp. 288–289.

7. John Gray, *Liberalism* (Minneapolis: University of Minnesota Press, 1986), p. 69.

8. *Ibid.*, p. 72.

9. Alexis de Tocqueville, *Democracy in America* (ed. Richard D. Heffner) (New York: New American Library, 1963).

10. John Dewey, *Liberalism and Social Action* (New York: Capricorn, 1963). Quoted in Leonard Peikoff, *The Ominous Parallels* (New York: Stein and Day, 1982).

11. *Ibid.*

12. John Dewey, *Reconstruction in Philosophy* (1920) (Boston: Beacon Press), pp. 194–195.

13. John Dewey, *Freedom and Culture* (New York: G.P. Putnam's Sons, 1939), p. 33.

14. Dewey, op. cit.

15. Richard Hofstadter, *The Age of Reform: From Bryan to F.D.R.* (New York: Vintage Books, 1955).

16. Bragdon, Henry W. and Samuel P. McCutchen, *History of a Free People* (New York: Macmillan), 1967, p. 510.

17. *Ibid.*, p. 514

18. See my discussion of the politics of victimization in *The Other Side of Racism* (Columbus: Ohio State University Press, 1981). See also John Murray Cuddihy's discussion of groups competing for status as "top underdog" in his *The Ordeal of Civility* (New York: Dell Publishing Co., 1974), p. 122.

19. This is not to say that a free and open society would be without conflicts of interest. In such a society those with less will want to acquire more, and those with more will want to keep what they have while obtaining more. There is no *necessary* conflict of interest in this, but since men are neither morally perfect nor omniscient, there is always the possibility that people will attempt to achieve gains by imposing their will on others through direct or indirect coercion. But in a free society men could not rely with impunity on physical or legislative coercion to realize their desires. Disparate interests may also come into conflict by virtue of noncoercive practices such as lying, deception, breach of promise, etc. But unless those acts involve the exchange of material values or the obstruction of justice, they are beyond the scope of the law to resolve. (Although consensus is not a necessary condition of a free society, nonviolent coexistence is.)

20. Ayn Rand, *Philosophy: Who Needs It* (New York: Bobbs-Merrill, 1982), p. 205.

21. By "just inequalities" I do not mean, as John Rawls does, inequalities in wealth, power, and authority that are justified to the extent that they work to the advantage of the worst off rather than those who are talented and socially advantaged. Inequalities in wealth, power, and authority are justified only to the extent that they are not the consequence of the use of force or fraud.

He Gains Who Serves Best

BY PAUL L. POIROT

"THE BEST offense is a good defense" may be effective strategy in war and various competitive sports to decide winners and losers. But this offense-defense terminology is misleading with reference to free market competition. Voluntary exchange is neither a game nor a war; it is a form of cooperation between buyer and seller to their mutual advantage—as each one determines advantage. So, the rule of the market would run more like this: "He gains most who serves best." A businessman's profits are a measure of his efficiency in the use of scarce and valuable resources to satisfy the most urgent wants of consumers.

Having competed successfully in the market, a property owner seeks to preserve his gains. But the market continues to insist: "He gains most who serves best." In other words, the way to preserve your gains is to keep on serving consumers efficiently; that's the only protection of property the market can offer.

It should be noted here that the market recognizes and accommodates numerous forms of property. Perhaps the most crucial and significant form is the individual's property right in his own person—his freedom to use as he pleases for any peaceful purpose his own ideas and energies and other faculties and possessions. As a self-owning, self-responsible human being, he is free to choose work or leisure, thrift or prodigality, specialization and trade or self-subsistence, formal education or on-his-own, splendor or plain living—anything peaceful, at his own expense. The market is there to serve him to the extent that he serves others: "He gains most who serves best."

In addition to one's right to his own life, the market recognizes and respects other forms of private property. There is the land, the space one occupies to the exclusion of others who have not earned access or been freely invited to share that space. There are the man-made buildings and tools of

---

Reprinted from *The Freeman* 25, no. 5 (May 1975).

further production. There is food, clothing, shelter, transportation, medical and dental care, news and other information, books, education, recreation, entertainment, services ranging from strictly unskilled manual labor to the most highly skilled professional help. All these are forms of private property, things owned and controlled by individuals as a consequence of peaceful production and trade—voluntary market transactions, according to the market formula: "He gains most who serves best."

A Wealthy Nation

Those who speak of the United States as a wealthy nation really mean that the citizens of this nation are relatively well off. And we should add the appropriate qualifications: (1) some of the citizens of the United States own more property than do others, and (2) the typical United States citizen owns more property than the typical citizen of other countries.

Without those qualifying conditions, the reference to a wealthy United States might be misconstrued as meaning that our federal government has unlimited resources at its command—an all-too-common belief.

Perhaps the people of the so-called underdeveloped Third World might be excused for the notion that the wealth of the United States is primarily in the form of government property. Citizens of lands long committed to communism have less reason to believe that the path to prosperity and happiness is through government ownership and control of resources. But what could be our excuse, we taxpayers of the United States, for possibly thinking of Uncle Sam as the source of endless goodies? Either our government is independently wealthy and has no need for taxpayers, or else it is dependent on taxpayers for its resources. Is there really any question about that?

Unfortunately, many citizens of the United States seem to be in doubt as to which is the case. They vote themselves instant protection and welfare, payable from Federal funds, as if there were no tomorrow—no accompanying tax burdens and disruption of business and trade. The facts to the contrary are announced daily in the various taxes added to purchases, weekly or bi-weekly in the list of deductions from pay checks, annually as income tax reports are filed. We have every reason to know there is a tax to pay for every act of government, whether to defend life and property and maintain peace and assure justice, or to transfer property from one person to another for whatever reason.

Why Some Have More

Because the market rewards individuals according to services rendered, the result is that some persons earn and own more property than do others. Strictly by serving the masses of mankind, some individuals have been made extremely wealthy. They have been given stewardship over vast amounts of property because of their proven capacity to use such scarce resources efficiently in providing the goods and services most sought and most valued by others. But if, for some reason, any present owner of scarce resources loses his touch, fails to serve efficiently, the open competition of the ongoing market process soon will bid the property into the hands of some new owner who serves better.

Meanwhile, the market process sustains vast numbers of us who pretend to know better than we do—who feign a wisdom not manifest in our performances. And one version of such "wisdom" holds that "we" know better than "they" how to use their property, that there is a more humane and just method of allocating scarce and valuable resources than to leave it to the market decisions of competing owners of private property. In other words, property should be redistributed "to each according to need," not left to the market rule: "He gains most who serves best." And just how is the market to be closed? Forcibly! Instead of upholding the dignity and property rights of the peaceful owner, the government shall intervene sometimes to drag a supplier unwillingly to market, sometimes to bar or limit his entry; sometimes to protect present owners of property in uses long since declared wasteful by any reasonable measure of the market place, sometimes to forcibly transfer property from the most efficient users into the hands of those who most miserably have failed to serve others in any way whatsoever.

The Best System

So we come back once more to the only rule the market follows, "He gains most who serves best." Despite the inequalities of wealth resulting from observance of that rule, no one reasonably contends that there is a better formula for human action in society. There is nothing morally wrong about voluntarily serving others. A person does not rationally contend that he has been impoverished because others have acted to serve his most urgent wants. When two parties voluntarily exchange their privately owned resources or properties, each gains—else he would not trade; and no uninvolved third party is harmed by reason of the trade.

While the rule of the market allows the greatest gain to the one who serves best, it affords no protection for any gain except through continuing use in the efficient service of others. In other words, the market insists that scarce resources be owned by those who are most proficient in serving willing customers, which is the least wasteful social distribution of wealth that is possible. To arbitrarily or coercively change the market-derived pattern of ownership is to introduce waste; and there is no historical or theoretically sound evidence that waste of scarce resources is socially beneficial. What any waste of any scarce resource amounts to in the final analysis is a waste of human lives—the inevitable consequence when compulsory collectivism interferes with or displaces the market process of open competition.

It is comforting to be a citizen of a wealthy nation. But a nation is wealthy only by reason of the fact that resources are privately owned and controlled according to the rule, "He gains most who serves best." And the only way in which government can usefully serve such a society is to keep the market open, restrain and punish those who violate the rule, but otherwise let free men compete.